30 DAYS TO
Taming
YOUR
Emotions

Deborah Smith Pegues

HARVEST HOUSE PUBLISHERS
EUGENE, OREGON

Cover by Koechel Peterson & Associates, Inc., Minneapolis, Minnesota

Cover photos © Thinkstock

30 DAYS TO TAMING YOUR EMOTIONS
Copyright © 2012 by Deborah Smith Pegues
Published by Harvest House Publishers
Eugene, Oregon 97402
www.harvesthousepublishers.com

Library of Congress Cataloging-in-Publication Data
Pegues, Deborah Smith, 1950-
    30 days to taming your emotions / Deborah Smith Pegues.
      p. cm.
    ISBN 978-0-7369-4825-8 (pbk.)
    ISBN 978-0-7369-4826-5 (eBook)
    1. Emotions—Religious aspects—Christianity. 2. Self-control—Religious aspects—Christianity. I. Title.
II. Title: Thirty days to taming your emotions.
    BV4597.3.P44 2012
    248.4—dc23
                                    2011036484

Printed in the United States of America

12 13 14 15 16 17 18 19 20 / BP-NI / 10 9 8 7 6 5 4 3 2

This book is dedicated to all my faithful readers. Your passion for learning and applying the Word to your lives inspires me to seek higher heights and deeper depths in God. Thank you for the motivation.

Contents

Introduction

■ ■ ■ ■

Julie was overwhelmed with debilitating emotions. Management seemed to have overlooked a host of more qualified junior executives and asked her to present a proposal to one of the company's most important clients. She'd convinced herself that flubbing this opportunity could spell the death of her career. Such an assumption caused her already sagging confidence to dip even lower. She was on edge and snapped at everyone who had gotten in her way the morning of the presentation. By the time she reached the boardroom where the meeting was to be held, her entire attitude reeked of negativity. Needless to say, her performance did not prove to be her finest hour. Her emotions had controlled her every move.

Emotions are the locomotive in our lives. Every decision we make is driven by a positive or negative emotion. In fact, the root meaning of the word emotion is "to move." Unfortunately, most people are moved primarily by their negative emotions. There are over 3,000 words in the language that describe our negativity. With such a vast array of options, I have chosen in the following pages to limit our focus to three common negative emotions that plague the masses: insecurity, stress, and damaging attitudes. Each of these is often a state of the mind that can derail your destiny and diminish your quality of life. But here's the good news: You don't have to be at the mercy of your emotions.

This book will show you how to recognize and confront your emotions and bring them into focus. No, I will not attempt to turn you into a clone of Mr. Spock, the emotionless Vulcan in the *Star Trek* television series. Emotions come with being human; controlling them comes with being born of the Spirit and giving Him free rein in our lives.

Throughout the following pages I want to challenge you to keep an open mind and be willing to change. Learning specialist Dr. Caroline Leaf says, "Behavior starts with a thought. Thoughts stimulate emotions which then result in attitude and finally produce behavior. Toxic thoughts produce toxic emotions, which produce toxic attitudes, resulting in toxic behaviors." Thoughts. Emotions. Attitude. Behavior. Yes, we can control every step of the process. Let's get started!

Day 1

Building a Firm Foundation

Resting on God's Word

■ ■ ■ ■

Who is this uncircumcised Philistine that he
should defy the armies of the living God?

1 Samuel 17:26

God desires that His children not be anxious for anything. He wants us to rest on His Word. Entering that rest is the challenge every problem presents to us today, and it was the challenge that faced the Israelites when confronted with the supersized human called Goliath.

Fourteen generations before the battle with Goliath, God gave Abraham His word about how He would take care of him. He promised, "I will bless those who bless you, and whoever curses you I will curse" (Genesis 12:3). Later, when He extended this and a host of other promises to Abraham's descendants, God inserted a key provision:

> This is my covenant with you and your descendants after you, the covenant you are to keep: Every male among you shall be circumcised. You are to undergo circumcision, and it will be the sign of the covenant between me and you (Genesis 17:10-11).

Abraham believed God's promises. So did David. David knew his circumcision made him an heir to the covenant. Thus, he could not help becoming righteously indignant when he came to the scene of the battle to bring food supplies and saw all of those circumcised Israelites running from the giant. Apparently no one remembered that the Jews had a covenant with God. He felt compelled to ask, "Who is this uncircumcised Philistine that he should defy the armies of the living God?" (1 Samuel 17:26).

David was in essence asking, "How could this man, who has no covenant with God, even think about conquering us?" Sadly, in fleeing from the giant, the Israelites proved that they had no confidence in that covenant. Can you relate to their action? How strong is your faith in God's promise to bless, protect, and prosper those who are in right standing with Him? If we continue to run from the giants in our lives, we will never see the power of God manifested.

Goliath had taunted the Israelites for 40 days before David came on the scene. Had any of the soldiers, including King Saul, their leader, believed the covenant, they could have taken care of Goliath themselves.

When you believe God's promises, you do not have to tolerate any giant in your life. We are heirs to the same covenant that God gave to Abraham. "If you belong to Christ, then you are Abraham's seed, and heirs according to the promise" (Galatians 3:29). How long have you tolerated the giant of insecurity? Do you believe that "God is able to bless you abundantly, so that in *all* things at *all* times, having *all* that you need, you will abound in *every* good work" (2 Corinthians 9:8, emphasis added)? Or have you chosen to let insecurity reign in your life and keep you from pursuing your goals or from having meaningful, trusting relationships? Left unchecked, insecurity will become a stronghold that will influence everything you do.

Too many of God's children think the Bible is not really for today, that many of its promises are now antiquated. They are sadly mistaken. David rested on a promise of protection that was 14 generations old, and it is still good today. The Word of God endures forever; there are no expiration dates on His promises. We must be diligent to hide them in our heart. For every project I embark on, I print out and memorize or refer often to passages from the Bible that remind me that apart from God I can do nothing and that He is faithful to complete whatever work He starts in me. For me, such Scriptures take the focus, the weight, and the responsibility from me and put them on Him.

It is not enough, however, to simply memorize Scripture. There is a difference between learning the Word and resting on it. Rest implies that we have ceased our negative thoughts and speculations. Our minds have stopped the doubting, stopped rehearsing what-if scenarios, and stopped being influenced by present realities. Nothing is too hard for God. He said so Himself. "I am the LORD, the God of all mankind. Is anything too hard for me?" (Jeremiah 32:27).

The story of David and Goliath is representative of many of the battles we face on a regular basis: good over evil, God's power over man's strength, and faith over fear. Whatever the situation, when the dust settles we are left with one abiding truth: We can rest on God's Word. "Now we who have believed enter that rest, just as God has said" (Hebrews 4:3).

Try writing out and memorizing the following personalized paraphrased version of 2 Corinthians 9:8, noting the emphasized words.

> God is able to bless me abundantly, so that I, in *all* things at *all* times, having *all* that I need, will abound in *every* good work.

Make a conscious decision to rest on these words in the coming weeks. Share them with a friend.

Securing Your Foundation

■ ■ ■ ■

The one who hears my words and does not put them into practice is like a man who built a house on the ground without a foundation. The moment the torrent struck that house, it collapsed and its destruction was complete.

LUKE 6:49

No structure can withstand the winds of adversity without a solid foundation. Our lives are no different. We must build them on a firm foundation if we expect to withstand the innumerable pressures of daily living.

Our lives are very similar to a stool that has a base and four legs. The base is our spiritual foundation, which consists primarily of prayer and the Word of God. The legs represent the financial, relational, mental, and physical aspects of our lives. Each leg must be strongly connected to our spiritual base in order for it to stand and be strong. Not one leg can stand alone and disconnected.

For example, the financial leg must be managed according to biblical principles of giving, integrity, hard work, and so forth. If not, you will experience stressful situations, such as too much debt, bad business deals, and fiscal chaos. The relational leg must also be handled according to biblical principles or we will not have the power to exercise unconditional love, forgiveness, or longsuffering. Our mental well-being is directly proportional to the extent to which we embrace God's Word and allow it to regulate our minds and emotions—and keep us in perfect peace. A strongly connected physical leg empowers us to treat our bodies according to the principles of the Word; we get proper rest, eat right, and engage in overall health maintenance. You get the picture. The strength and success of every facet of our lives will be determined by the strength of our foundation. If the base is weak, there is no hope for the legs.

It is no wonder, then, that Satan makes every attempt to prevent us from strengthening our base. We must be diligent to secure our foundation first thing each day before we fall victim to distractions. I remember one day when I was preparing to pray. I went into my prayer room, and just as I started to pray I decided it would really be nice to listen to my sounds of nature CD that featured birds chirping, running streams, and background music. It would be a great backdrop for prayer as well as a de-stressor as I would imagine being alone with the Lord in a forest— especially if I used my noise-blocking headphones. When I went to the place where I normally kept these items, I could not find the headphones or the CD. I searched everywhere. In one room I looked through a stack of CDs that were waiting to be put back into their original cases. I figured that since I was there I'd take a quick minute to organize them. Fifteen minutes later I moved from there and proceeded to look in the trunk of my car for the missing items. There I found another array of CDs that needed to be organized and put back into their original cases. I thought, *Oh, what's an extra ten minutes? I'll make it up to the Lord.* I organized the CDs—and the entire trunk. Next I went into my home office and behold, there they were—my noise-blocking headphones and my nature CD. But since I was so close to the computer, I decided to quickly check my e-mail just in case there was one that needed an urgent reply. I have friends who jokingly describe this set of distractions as AAADD—Age-Activated Attention Deficit Disorder.

Nevertheless, an hour later, I was now ready to head back to my prayer room. Of course, the hour I had scheduled to pray was up, so I ended up spending about 20 hurried, guilt-filled minutes running through my prayer list and quickly browsing through a psalm. I thought, *How rude of me to start a conversation with the Lord and then leave Him hanging for an entire hour!* Would I have done that to anyone else? Of course not. But the day was waiting and I was already behind on my to-do list. I knew that even the 20 minutes I had spent were better than nothing, but I did not feel I had really nourished my spirit. I did not feel I had made the level of connection I desired. Rather, I felt the accuser trying to convince me that I had only been performing an obligatory duty. I am "supposed" to pray because I am a Bible teacher, and teachers should be able to say that they pray consistently.

The only way I have found to be consistent in prayer is to set a specific time and place for it. Otherwise, something else will keep taking precedence over it. Do not allow yourself to be distracted. Do not fool yourself into thinking you will get to it later. By the end of the day, you'll be too tired to enter into His rest. You'll simply want to say, "God, bless everybody in the whole world. You know their needs. Good night!"

I believe a time will come in every Christian's life when the key to their survival will depend on their relationship with the Lord. When my friend Althea Sims' husband suffered a massive stroke, she suddenly found herself thrust into the role of holding together—spiritually and administratively—the church where he was pastor. She also had to assume responsibility for their household finances—a task he had always handled. These were uncharted waters for her. Further, she had to continue her duties as mother to her dependent children.

The doctors provided little hope of Pastor Reggie's survival during the days following his stroke. Althea was the Rock of Gibraltar and it was not a facade—you could feel her strength and her peace. Recently I asked her how she kept her sanity during that extremely stressful period. She responded, "I survived because of where I was in the Lord when it all happened." She had secured her foundation way before the storm. Solomon was right when he said, "If you fail under pressure, your strength is not very great" (Proverbs 24:10). We cannot escape life's troubles or stressors, but we can fortify our spirits with prayer and the Word of God so that we can have the strength and courage to respond to and overcome them.

Fighting Prayerlessness

■ ■ ■ ■

Men always ought to pray and not lose heart.

LUKE 18:1 NKJV

The remora fish is a great role model of the importance of staying connected to a source bigger and more powerful than ourselves. This fish has an oval sucking disk on the top of its head that allows it to attach itself to the underside of other large fish or sea vessels. The shark is its favorite host. Once it attaches to the shark, the remora does not have to concern itself with daily issues such as food, transportation, or safety. It feeds on the food that falls from the shark's mouth as it devours its prey. Of course, the remora has the option of swimming on its own, but when it decides to connect to the shark, it goes where the shark goes. It does not attempt to go in an opposite direction. Protection? It is a nonissue for one who is connected to such a powerful and fearless creature. Inadequacy? No way! The remora knows the shark can carry it to places it could never go alone.

Hmmm, doesn't this sound like the relationship God desires to have with His children? He wants us to feed on the Word that comes out of His mouth. He wants us to follow Him where He leads and not to take off on independent excursions, assuming He will tag along. He wants us to live with the assurance that He will protect not only our lives, but also our relationships and all that pertains to us. Oh, that we would emulate the remora. We would then find ourselves securing our connection to God on a daily basis through prayer. He is waiting to carry us to places we could never go alone.

Prayer connects us to this inexhaustible Source that supplies our every need. Unfortunately, too many people wait until a crisis forces them to make the connection. The prophet Isaiah admonished the Jewish leaders to "pray day and night, continually. Take no rest, all you who pray to the LORD. Give the LORD no rest" (Isaiah 62:6-7 NLT). It is so easy to slip into the habit of giving God too much rest. Being a schedule-driven person,

I find that I tend to be more consistent in prayer when I use the prayer guidelines that I established using the word "pray" as an acronym:

Pause. I stop all activity and focus completely on God. Worship is total preoccupation; we can only be preoccupied with one thing at a time. I understand many people pray while they exercise or drive to work. However, the greatest honor and respect we can give to anyone is our undivided attention. I slow my pace when I come into His presence. I breathe deeply and slowly. With each breath I absorb His holiness and His power. I have my prayer journal and a pen ready to record His thoughts to me throughout the time of prayer.

Reverence. I express my admiration for all His attributes. I hallow (make sacred; bless) His name. At this point, distractions start to pop up like dandelions. I will notice a dead leaf on a houseplant or something out of place in the room, or I will suddenly remember a task I need to put on my to-do list. I have learned to jot down the task in my journal and ignore the other issues for what they are—mere distractions that can be dealt with later. I have also learned that praying audibly helps to minimize wandering thoughts.

I come into His presence singing songs that exalt Him. I thank Him for all He has done and will do. I express several things I am particularly grateful for that day. I read and meditate on a passage of Scripture. I recommend that beginners read a chapter in the life of Jesus from one of the four Gospels, or a chapter from the book of Proverbs that corresponds with the date of the month (there are 31 chapters). Further reading options may include a chapter from the book of Acts, noting the power of the early church, or a Psalm. I personally enjoy studying particular subject matters, such as faith, forgiveness, pride, and so forth.

Ask. I ask for forgiveness of my sins, making every effort to be specific. I pray for the power to live a Christian life and ask God to give me a passion for His Word and for prayer. I ask for His will to be done in every aspect of my life: spiritually, physically, financially, relationally, vocationally, and emotionally. I pray for each one separately.

Using a prepared list, I ask for God's will to be done in the lives of my family members, friends, coworkers, neighbors, pastor and church, government, and others. Rather than launching into a "Let it be…" mode, I ask the Holy Spirit to make intercession for me according to the will of God.

Yield. I must subordinate my requests to God's sovereign will, trusting that He knows what is best. I strive to maintain a "nevertheless" attitude. Therefore, I am careful to conclude my prayer by saying, "Nevertheless, not my will, Lord, but Yours be done." I leave the prayer room knowing I have made the connection and have been refueled. God is always listening to the prayers of His children.

The old adage that it is not *what* you know but *whom* you know that gives you the advantage in a situation is true—especially from a spiritual perspective. When we have a relationship with God, we come to understand that He is sufficient to handle any demand placed upon us. That kind of confidence comes from knowing we are connected to omnipotence.

To develop good prayer habits, start with a 15-minute commitment to prayer for five days per week. Further, take mini-praise breaks throughout each day and make faith-building declarations such as:

"Lord, I thank You that You are with me."

"Father, You are awesome. Nothing is too hard for You."

"Thank You for life, health, strength, wisdom, and a sound mind."

Day 2

Managing Your Body

The Role of Sleep

■ ■ ■ ■

I will lie down in peace and sleep, for you
alone, LORD, make me dwell in safety.

PSALM 4:8

Sleep is just as important to our survival as water and food. Getting sufficient sleep to restore our bodies is a key factor in coping with day-to-day stress. Further, failure to get enough sleep also increases stress and can make us less able to handle stressful situations. Most adults, regardless of age, need the recommended eight hours of restful sleep a night. But sometimes stress can keep us awake, making matters worse as we find ourselves in a vicious cycle of a stressful situation keeping us up and then a lack of sleep causing more stress. Sleeplessness, then, can be one of many signs that our body is under stress.

What about your sleep habits? Do you have a sleep routine in which you go to bed and get up at about the same time, or do you allow events, people, deadlines, or other circumstances to dictate your sleep schedule? For those of you whose bedtime routine is rather extensive, do you start to wind down in plenty of time to allow yourself to complete it, or does the routine itself become a stressor? Ever thought about completing it hours before your bedtime?

Most of us think of sleep as some passive process in which we drift off into oblivion and wake up several hours later well rested. The truth of the matter is that sleep is an active state. Many metabolic and other restorative processes occur during the various stages of sleep. If we do not sleep long enough for our system to be rejuvenated, we will most likely find ourselves irritated by the smallest things and battling a whale of an appetite. The excess hunger is just our body's cry for the energy that was supposed to be supplied by a good night's sleep.

If you have trouble sleeping, you can try some things to help you sleep better. Although experts say that you should not exercise within a couple of hours of turning in, I find that a leisurely walk on my treadmill helps me to sleep well. The key is not to engage in an activity that raises your heart rate significantly because that will interfere with sleep. You might also try taking a warm bath while burning an aromatherapy candle. You will want to avoid caffeine, alcohol, nicotine, and heavy meals near bedtime. (Of course, eliminating the consumption or use of these things in general would be a plus.) If you are menopausal or premenopausal, you might need to add sugar to this list. You will want to make sure that your room is dark and cool. The purchase of blackout window shades to avoid the bright morning light would be a good investment. I use eyeshades so that the light doesn't disturb me when my husband arises before I get up. A good comfortable mattress and pillow are a must. Don't skimp here. They are as important as wearing comfortable shoes. I have a memory foam pillow that ensures the correct alignment of my head and body throughout the night. When I go on a trip, I notice the difference in my quality of sleep. Keep your bed linens fresh. Even if you do not change your sheets every few days, fresh pillowcases will still set the stage for a pleasant sleeping experience.

If you are unable to turn off your racing mind, try breathing deeply. If there is an issue that you need to deal with, then plan to do so. Get in touch with why you are unable to sleep.

If none of these suggestions work and you still have trouble sleeping for three weeks or longer, talk to your doctor, a sleep disorder specialist, or a mental health professional. In the meantime, continue to meditate on sleep-related Scriptures, such as Proverbs 3:24: "Yes, you will lie down and your sleep will be sweet" (NKJV). And keep praying to the great Great Physician.

Nourishing Your Body

■ ■ ■ ■

So whether you eat or drink or whatever
you do, do it all for the glory of God.

1 Corinthians 10:31

You will be able to manage your stress much more effectively if you know how the foods you consume affect your body's ability to cope with daily pressures. Despite the many books on the market today that adequately explain how to properly fuel our bodies, nutritional ignorance seems to be the norm in America as the rate of obesity continues to rise. When the pressure is on, many find refuge and comfort in food.

Nourishing our bodies properly is a lifelong endeavor, and we would do well to become as nutrition-conscious as possible. I am surprised by the number of people who do not know the difference between proteins (lean meats, eggs, etc.) and carbohydrates (breads, pastas, potatoes, rice, etc.). Some are oblivious to the difference between *simple* carbohydrates (man-manipulated stuff, like chips, cookies, and cakes) and *complex* carbohydrates (fruit, vegetables, legumes, and foods that have not been altered by man). Complex carbohydrates and proteins are a winning combination to a healthy body and proper weight management. Finally, there are some who think that "cholesterol free" means that the cooking oils are calorie free and can be consumed in unlimited quantities versus the reality that it is simply unsaturated (won't go solid when cold) but has the same number of calories—which are the highest of all food choices. You can improve your nutritional IQ by going to your local bookstore or health food store and buying books or even pocket booklets that explain the composition of certain foods. Once you understand that there are virtually no nutrients in junk foods, you cannot in good conscience make a steady diet of them. Sure, you may crave an occasional Twinkie, but eating them regularly should not be part of your food regimen.

If you have the physical stress symptoms of poor concentration, fatigue, or a ferocious appetite, you may be tempted to get a quick fix by eating junk food. The items of choice usually contain caffeine, sugar, or something salty with a crunch. Do you find it interesting that when spelled backward, s-t-r-e-s-s-e-d is d-e-s-s-e-r-t-s? Have you noticed that you never tend to crave foods like carrots, apples, or lean meats, even though they may be better for you in the long run? But therein is the answer: the long run. It takes a healthy food choice longer to raise our blood sugar to the point where we feel satisfied, whereas the junk food delivers an immediate result because its refined ingredients are quickly assimilated. Further, they cause your brain to release serotonin, a hormone that helps you to relax—for a brief time. The time is so brief that you'll need another hit of carbohydrates to recover from the precipitous drop in your blood sugar. This time you'll probably have to consume even more carbohydrates because your blood sugar drops even lower than it was originally after the first carbohydrate fix, so your body is going to have to work harder to get your sugar level back to normal.

Is this beginning to sound like a drug addiction scenario? Through all of this activity, there is a good chance that you are not really hungry, but rather feeding whatever emotion (anger, fear, fatigue, etc.) the stress generated. A 10- to 15-minute nap may be the best solution. Of course, if you were diligent to make sure that you ate the right foods frequently throughout the day, your blood sugar would stay at a level that would eliminate those cravings.

Learn your own body and monitor what triggers you to want to eat. One of the best strategies against stressful eating is to get the healthy protein in your system first thing in the morning. Rather than donuts and coffee, try having an egg sandwich or peanut butter and toast with low-fat or soy milk. Plan for times when you may be prone to stressful eating by having only healthy alternatives available. When I go away to write, I only stock foods that are healthy to eat. Of course, I hate it at midnight when I feel I could eat a whole bag of Oreos but only have cantaloupe available!

Nutritional and homeopathic supplements also play a vital role in helping us to cope with stress, tension, or anxiety. However, before you begin an herbal program, you should at least make a call to your medical doctor to make sure that certain herbs do not interfere with your current medications. It is a known fact that during times of stress, more vitamin C is depleted from the body. Therefore, an extra dose to replenish it may be needed.

Our food choice habits took years to develop. I can trace my propensity to reach for sugar back to my grandmother's house, where her tea cakes made everything better when I had a problem. Now, just because I have identified the source of the bad habit does not mean I can continue to use it to justify bad behavior. It simply means I have to develop new coping habits for my life. For example, most of the time I now try to opt for a piece of fruit or a small protein bar instead of a refined carbohydrate snack that has little or no nutrients.

Prolonged stress can cause our internal systems to break down. We need to keep our insides strong by selecting foods that nourish us rather than work against us.

Getting Physical

■ ■ ■ ■

I discipline my body like an athlete, training it
to do what it should. Otherwise, I fear that after
preaching to others I myself might be disqualified.

1 Corinthians 9:27 nlt

Physical activity is an excellent stress-buster and is critical to normalizing your body after a stressful event. When your brain senses a threat or danger, it quickly releases hormones carrying an urgent message via the bloodstream to the adrenal glands (which sit atop the kidneys). The message says, "Let's prepare to resist or to run now!" The adrenal glands produce excess stress chemicals, cortisol and adrenaline, and rush them into the bloodstream, where they get delivered to various parts of the body via nerve fibers. The body responds with increased strength, raised blood pressure, and other assistance needed to resist or run. There have been countless stories of people who exhibited unusual strength in a crisis. I heard of a petite young mother who actually lifted the back of a car under which her child had been trapped.

Of course, a crisis is not limited to threats of physical danger. The threat of losing a job or a loved one, or even the excitement of a happy occasion, can cause the brain to put the body on high alert. The adrenal glands do not attempt to distinguish between negative or positive excitement.

Once the crisis is over, the excess hormones need to be dissipated out of the bloodstream. This is where exercise plays a critical role. Regular physical activity helps to burn these extra chemicals so your body can return to normal. Imagine their buildup if you tend to live in a period of stress day in and day out. Studies have linked an accumulation of stress hormones to strokes, heart disease, high blood pressure, thyroid malfunction, decrease in muscle tissue, obesity, impaired memory, and a host of other maladies. In fact, people have died from heart failure in a crisis because their heart muscle was not strong enough to handle all of the stress hormones that had been pumped into the bloodstream to prepare the body to handle the crisis.

In addition to its positive impact on stress, physical activity provides us with numerous other benefits, including better resistance to illness, stronger bones, more energy, and stronger muscles. What activity is best? The best form of exercise is the one you enjoy and find the most convenient.

These are the two biggest reasons why most of us fail to be consistent in following an exercise program. First, we might lose interest in the activity because we don't really get a lot of satisfaction out of doing it. I have had beginning lessons in almost every sport—two or three times for some. Rollerblading, skiing, swimming, golfing, and even completing the Los Angeles Marathon have not held my interest. I'm just a plain walker. I get great joy from bonding with my friends as we power walk or even stroll through various parks, neighborhood walking routes, and beach paths.

Secondly, we tend to not be consistent in an activity if it requires too much time or effort to access. Why join a gym across town and only show up two or three times a year? Exercising already requires discipline, so why allow inconvenience to add more stress to the process?

Whether a brisk walk or a high-energy fitness class, almost any physical activity will help you let off steam, distract you from your source of stress, and improve your mood. It also relaxes and reenergizes your body. The duration of the exercise should be a minimum of 30 minutes of physical activity a day at least five days a week. Doing more is even better. Some fitness gurus suggest that if you cannot carve out 30 minutes at a time, grab 10-minute segments throughout the day.

There are also other benefits to making exercise the center of your stress-busting program. People who are routinely active tend to eat better, and as discussed in the previous section, a healthy diet also helps your body manage stress better. In addition, physical activity can help you lose weight, keep it off, and feel better about yourself. Feeling physically inadequate can be a stressor in itself.

If you cannot find the time for an official workout, try building the activity into your lifestyle. My doctor recently suggested that I park on the outskirts of the shopping mall so that I will be forced to walk farther. You may try taking the stairs several times during the day for a certain number of floors.

Stress can wear your body down mentally and physically; however, a healthy body can cope with stress better than an unhealthy one. In 1 Timothy 4:8, Paul reminded Timothy, "Physical exercise is of some value, but godliness has value for all things, holding promise for both the present life and the life to come."

Tailor your physical activities to your lifestyle. The most important thing is to keep moving.

Day 3

A Job Half Done

The Apathetic Attitude

■ ■ ■ ■

Lack of interest or concern regarding problems of others

I heard a story about a high school social studies teacher who, frustrated with the apathy of his students, stormed into the classroom one day and with great indignation wrote A-P-A-T-H-Y on the board in huge letters and placed an exclamation point behind it. He wrote so hard, the chalk broke. Two students, who had been forced to sit in the front row because they had arrived too late for the ever popular seats in the back of the room, looked at him with their normal disinterest. One of them cocked his head to the side and asked his classmate, "What is ah-pay-thigh?" His friend responded, "Who cares?"

Does this sound like your attitude? Are you so focused on your own life that nothing much else matters? Let's look at some factors that may be numbing your compassion, enthusiasm, and motivation.

Lack of Goals. You fall into apathy when your desires stop and you have no target for your energies. What used to excite you? What killed your interest in it? Is it a desire you could rekindle? Go ahead and write down something—anything—that you could start to pursue now. Forget about the potential cost or all the reasons why the idea or activity might not work. Just give your mind the luxury of feeling hopeful and excited about something, even a small thing.

Wrong Goals. Your general lack of motivation could be because you are pursuing a goal imposed upon you by someone else, such as working toward a degree in a subject you hate. Or like Jonah before he was swallowed by the great fish, maybe you are rowing against the tide of God's will for your life. Have you checked in with the Almighty lately to see if this may be so? Did He really lead you to indulge in that luxury item that is now requiring you to work two jobs? Or maybe the time has ended for a goal that was part of God's plan for a certain season of your life. Moving on is sometimes hard, but oh, the joy and peace of knowing you are in the center of His perfect will.

Spiritual Apathy. If your love for God has waned, then it follows that you will not be concerned about the things that concern Him. Bob Pierce, founder of World Vision (a Christian humanitarian organization that fights poverty and injustice for children and their communities around the world), once prayed, "Let my heart be broken by the things that break the heart of God." Loving and caring for our neighbor is among God's top priorities.

In responding to the question "Who is my neighbor?" Jesus told a group of Jewish lawyers a parable (Luke 10:25-37). In the story, a Jew on his way to Jericho was attacked by thieves and left half-dead on the side of the road. A priest came along, saw his plight, and retreated to the other side. A Levite, a priest's helper, came along and responded likewise. Finally, a Samaritan, though a hated outsider, saw the man's condition and showed compassion. He dressed his wounds, took him to a local inn, and paid in advance for a few nights' stay. Jesus proceeded to explain that loving God ought to make us love our neighbor—and our neighbor is anyone who needs us.

But why did the priest and the Levite demonstrate such apathy? We can only surmise that they were too focused on their own agendas. Or maybe they were overwhelmed with the magnitude of the problem and didn't want to commit the time and the resources necessary to get the man back on his feet.

I used to feel overwhelmed when I would hear stories of millions of starving children in the world. Then someone convinced me to sponsor one impoverished child in another country. I believe that because of my support, she will impact many. Whatever your reason for doing nothing, it is unacceptable to God. "If anyone has material possessions and sees a brother or sister in need but has no pity on them, how can the love of God be in that person? Dear children, let us not love with words or speech but with actions and in truth" (1 John 3:17-18). The admonition is simple: "Do something!"

There is nothing more personally rewarding than serving others. Unfortunately, if you have lost your passion for life, you'll be hard-pressed to improve the quality of life for someone else. That's why you must wage an offensive against apathy starting this very moment. For each category below, list one doable goal you believe you can pursue and complete within the next two weeks:

Spiritual goal: _____

(*Example:* Pray 15 minutes as soon as you awaken each day for government, church, family, and other concerns.)

Relational goal: _____

(*Example:* Join an online social network, and reconnect with old friends.)

Physical goal: _____

(*Example:* Go for a three-mile walk; ask a few others to join you.)

Professional goal: _____

(*Example:* Become proficient at Microsoft Word by completing the free online tutorial.)

The examples I've given you are all simple activities that can get you moving toward a goal. They require no money, only a commitment to do them. Reignite your passion for life. There are people out there who need what God has deposited in you, and you need what He has deposited in them. It is time to get out of neutral and shift into drive!

The Fatalistic Attitude

■ ■ ■ ■

Believing all things and events are
inevitable and determined by fate

"Well, there's no sense in undergoing all those special treatments. If I'm going to die from this disease, I'm going to die. Que sera, sera; whatever will be, will be."

Perhaps you have heard someone express this attitude when faced with a difficult life decision. The belief that the events of our lives are predetermined, set in stone, and beyond our control is called fatalism—and it is not biblical although certain Scriptures seem to imply support for this concept. For example, Psalm 139:16 (NLT) declares,

> You saw me before I was born.
> Every day of my life was recorded in your book.
> Every moment was laid out
> before a single day had passed.

Do you think this is a license to live your life with no personal responsibility for how it turns out? Absolutely not! God has made us stewards not only over our money but over every aspect of our lives. Do you really believe that since God has determined the number of days that you will live you have no obligation to ensure the *quality* of those days by taking care of your body or maintaining healthy relationships with others?

A fatalistic attitude can lead to a sense of resignation about life and rob you of godly ambition and enthusiasm about the future. "If I can't change destiny, then why bother trying?" While God in His foreknowledge knows every decision we will make from cradle to grave, He has not predetermined them. He has given every person a free will. Even where we will spend eternity will be based upon the choices we make. These choices include not only making Jesus Lord over our lives but also a decision to embrace the Word of God as the foundation and reference point for every aspect of our existence.

In describing the great white throne judgment we all will face, John reported, "And I saw the dead, small and great, standing before the throne, and books were opened. Another book was opened, which is the book of life. And the dead were judged *according to what they had done* as recorded in the book" (Revelation 20:12, emphasis added).

Yes, God is sovereign and rules in the affairs of men. I believe He has designed a wonderful plan for my life and yours. If we acknowledge Him and submit to His guidance, we will fulfill our divine destiny. However, being human, we are subject to doing things according to our own understanding and veering from His ordained path.

In times like these, God, because of His love and mercy, responds in a manner similar to a GPS. On a recent road trip, I programmed my car's GPS for my destination. However, on the way there I got a bright idea for a quick shopping detour and made an unscheduled turn. The automated GPS voice immediately said, "Recalculating…" and proceeded to tell me how to get back on the path that would get me to my original destination. No, the brakes on the car did not lock, neither did the alarm sound. I simply had to make a choice to ignore or heed the new instructions.

Is there a circumstance in your life that you have surrendered to fate? Perhaps you've said, "I'm destined to be fat; it's in my genes!" "It's not in the cards for me to have financial abundance." "I'm just shy; that's how God made me." Don't let your fatalistic attitude sentence you to a life of excuses, frustration, and mediocrity.

Yes, God has set the framework of your life, but He has given you a wide range of freedoms within that framework. Like a GPS, God knows exactly where you are in life and what you need to do to fulfill your divine destiny. Why not stop right now and acknowledge an area where your fatalism is reigning unchecked? Ask God to give you a specific strategy for overcoming this mindset.

The Mediocre Attitude

■ ■ ■ ■

*Tendency to be satisfied with average
or slightly inferior results*

The housekeeper slid the dust cloth around the edges of the stack of books on the table; however, she failed to pick up the stack and clean away the dirt underneath. *That'll do,* she thought, and she went on to the next task.

Later that evening, when the owner sat down to read, he accidentally upset the stack of books and they all tumbled to the floor. As he began to restack them, he noticed the outline of the undusted area. "Good help is hard to find," he sighed with resignation.

Mediocrity had struck again. It has become the norm in our society.

As I write this, the anesthesia from my outpatient surgery earlier today has pretty much worn off. The hospital where the procedure was performed is under new management. When I entered the building this morning, I noticed several posted signs that implied excellence is the new order of the day. The attitudes of the sign-in security guard, the X-ray technicians, the nurses, the anesthesiologist who answered my endless questions, and everyone else I encountered demonstrated their quest for excellence and patient satisfaction. What a contrast to some of my prior experiences with certain other medical facilities.

Do you have a mediocre mindset regarding certain tasks? If so, consider the level of frustration you would experience if the people who served you had a "that'll do" attitude. What if your restaurant server delivered your food only partially cooked and your drink in a not-so-clean glass? Or what if your administrative assistant made a couple of comma corrections manually rather than keying in the corrections and reprinting the letter?

Notice how easy it is to get the picture when you think about other people's behavior?

Now hold up the mirror to your own actions. Are there any activities, assignments, or duties that you have approached with a "that'll do" mindset in your personal or professional life? For instance, are you thorough in researching a solution to a problem even if the answer lies outside your department or you may not receive credit or recognition for the results?

If you are ready to confront your mediocre attitude, the strategies below will get you onto your path to overcoming it.

Acknowledge specific areas where you have not been a model of excellence. Pray for God's intervention in your thinking so that you can begin to establish new norms in your life.

Pursue excellence rather than perfectionism. Perfectionism is just the need to be blameless. When you try to pass it off as a badge of excellence, you will find that the glory goes to you and your efforts and not to God. So avoid it. Excellence is about putting forth your very best to achieve your goal.

Realize that excellence takes time and extra effort. In fact, the "excel" in *excellence* implies that you must go beyond the norm.

I once hired an accountant who had such a mediocre attitude, I dreaded reviewing her bank reconciliations. She would allow outstanding checks and even the company's own deposits to remain in uncleared status for months without investigation. Also, when I taught accounting at a major university, I noticed some students learned only the mechanics of solving a problem but did not take the time to understand the theory behind the solution. They put themselves at a sore disadvantage.

I admit that I have a tendency to be mediocre about certain household chores. When rearranging pictures on the wall in our home, I usually hang the new picture right over the dust of the old one with the intention of cleaning it later. My husband, "Mr. Neat-so," insists on thoroughly cleaning the wall as well as the glass on the photo before hanging it—an often time-consuming undertaking. My goal, of course, like most people with a mediocre mindset toward an endeavor, is just to get done with the project and move on to the next thing.

Avoid people with poor work habits or who pooh-pooh your efforts to be excellent. Are they achieving the kinds of results you desire?

I've worked in several environments where the chief executive traveled extensively or was rarely in the office. The old adage "when the cat is away, the mice will play" was never more true. Invariably a coworker would give me a lecture about how "corporations are not loyal anymore," "life is too short to work so hard," "the weather is too great to be stuck inside," and a litany of other excuses to justify his mediocrity. I just kept right on working.

I have also had to be on guard in my personal life, especially as a married woman. I've had single friends or people who have given up on finding a lifetime partner scoff at my efforts to maintain the fire in my marriage. "You've snared him now, why are you doing all that?" they say. I ignore such comments. With over 32 years of marriage under our belts, Darnell and I still run for the mouthwash when we hear the other pull into the garage; we value a fresh kiss. He always opens my car door, sometimes in spite of my protests when it's raining or too cold and we're scurrying to get in the car. We have cultivated the habit of going the extra mile to support each other's efforts.

Aristotle said, "We are what we repeatedly do. Excellence, then, is not an act, but a habit."

Study or observe the lives of people who have excelled in their field. Learn and model their habits. You can start right now. Think of someone whose excellence you admire. Identify one of his character traits or habits you'd like to emulate (e.g., staying focused or persevering in the face of opposition). Understand how God rewards excellence:

> Do you see any truly competent workers?
> They will serve kings
> rather than working for ordinary people
> (Proverbs 22:29 NLT).

Don't tolerate mediocrity from people under your authority. This does not mean that you become a tyrant; rather, you simply set and model high standards. You must also have the courage to enforce appropriate consequences when those you lead fail to adhere to those standards. Results: increased self-esteem and greater respect from others.

Perform every assignment or endeavor as if God requested it and will be evaluating your performance. Out of sight, out of mind does not apply to God; He is mindful of your every activity. "Whatever you do, work heartily, as for the Lord and not for men, knowing that from the Lord you will receive the inheritance as your reward. You are serving the Lord Christ" (Colossians 3:23-24 ESV). This alone is the best reason to maintain your strong work ethic even when the boss is not around.

Day 4

Arresting Anger

The Sarcastic Attitude

■ ■ ■ ■

Tendency to use witty language to convey insults or scorn

Shortly before his execution by firing squad, the murderer James Rodgers was asked whether he had any final requests. "Why, yes," he replied. "I'd like a bulletproof vest." Even at the point of death, he could not resist sarcasm.

Do you regularly respond to others in a way that is opposite of what you really feel—as evidenced by your tone or body language (smirking, raising eyebrows, cocking your head to the side, sighing)? Sarcasm's goal is to scorn, belittle, insult, or express irritation or disapproval—and it can ruin your relationships. Still, you can find it in all social interactions. Here are a few examples:

At home: Junior brings in his report card, which reflects low grades in all subjects. Dad says, "Way to go, Einstein!" Dad is expressing his frustration by saying the opposite of what he's really feeling.

In sports: The rookie baseball player strikes out—for the third time. The coach yells, "Nice going, Jack!"

Romantic relationship: John buys his wife, Sue, a pair of small diamond earrings. Sue, who had hoped for larger gems, says, "Boy, these are really going to blind people!"

As a word of caution, sarcasm is not always wrong, and there are instances of its use even in the Bible. One of the most notable incidents occurred when Elijah challenged the false prophets of Baal to call down fire to prove who the real God was. He let them go first in putting a sacrifice on an altar and calling on their god to send down fire to consume it. After several hours of watching them call upon Baal with no results, Elijah became sarcastic. "At noon Elijah began to taunt them. 'Shout louder!' he said. 'Surely he is a god! Perhaps he is deep in thought, or busy, or traveling. Maybe he is sleeping and must be awakened'" (1 Kings 18:27). In this instance, Elijah justifiably used sarcasm to show the prophets of Baal the folly of worshipping a false god. God Himself used sarcasm when He ridiculed those who took a block of wood and used half of it for fuel and the other half to make a "god" (Isaiah 44:13-20).

How has your sarcastic attitude affected your life? How do you typically respond to your recurring frustrations or irritations with others? Perhaps you have convinced yourself that you are not sarcastic at all, just witty or clever. Sarcasm is no joke, despite your best attempt to disguise it with a laugh. Perhaps you are not aware that your sarcasm most likely leaves the hearer feeling diminished or devalued. This is no way to win friends or influence people. If you want to begin to address this poor communication style, the strategies below should help.

Admit your motive for being sarcastic. You may be attempting to control other people or to shame them out of behavior that you disapprove of. Face it, the only person whose behavior you can control is yourself. Or maybe you are trying to display your great intellect by calling attention to the deficiency of another.

Practice a more direct approach to expressing your displeasure. Posing a simple question designed to gain a better understanding will go a long way. For example, rather than asking "What in the world were you thinking?" try, "What strategy or goal did you have in mind when you made that move?" This latter statement expresses confidence that surely some forethought was applied. God will give you the right words to say if you ask Him to. "Those who are wise will find a time and a way to do what is right, for there is a time and a way for everything" (Ecclesiastes 8:5-6 NLT).

Consider the implications and consequences of what you are about to say before you say it. Ask yourself, "Will my words imply that the hearer is stupid or has poor judgment? Do they tear down or do they build?" "Do not let any unwholesome talk come out of your mouths, but only what is helpful for building others up according to their needs, that it may benefit those who listen" (Ephesians 4:29). Make sure every word passes the "benefit" test.

Consider how you would feel if someone were to say to you what you are about to say to another. Let the Golden Rule be your guide.

The Angry Attitude

▨ ▨ ▨ ▨

*Hostile; showing or feeling hatred, enmity
toward a person or group*

My friend Arbra Ezell, a Spirit-filled family counselor, passed away in 2008, but her words will live long in my memory, "Anger is a secondary emotion; you must identify the primary emotion that gave rise to it." These primary emotions are our internal responses we assign to external events. They include hurt, humiliation, disappointment, frustration, feeling disrespected, disregarded, overlooked, manipulated, and a host of other complex emotions.

Wouldn't it be great if we would just delay our emotional response to a negative event? For example, suppose several months ago you finalized your plans to celebrate your milestone wedding anniversary with a select group of couples. You've purchased theater tickets for the entire party of eight as an expression of your appreciation of your long-term friendship. The preshow dinner reservations have been made, and you are looking forward to a great time.

The day before the celebration, Couple X calls and informs you they have friends who are flying in unexpectedly and want to know if they can invite this couple to join the festivities. You immediately assign the emotion of *annoyance* to what you perceive as a negative event. You and your husband love Couple X dearly, but they have a pattern of making last-minute changes to established plans, which has often frustrated the close-knit group.

What are your choices now? You could advise Couple X that you are trying to create a memory with established friends and do not want the unfamiliar couple to join you, or you could agree to let them come and later display an angry attitude in your impatience with the wait staff at the restaurant, theater personnel, or even the unfamiliar couple.

This fairly harmless instance demonstrates how easily you can develop an angry attitude. By no means am I minimizing the more serious hurts that many have experienced at the hands of unwise parents, abusive spouses, mean bosses, and others. If you have been hurt in this way and have never brought closure by confronting these issues, you most likely developed an angry attitude toward those who remind you of the original painful event. When others observe this angry attitude, they can often be very judgmental about your behavior and seek to put distance in the relationship without putting forth the least bit of effort to understand your underlying pain.

What good is there in holding on to anger anyway? A wise person once said, "For every minute you're angry, you lose sixty seconds of happiness." An angry attitude thwarts your personal and professional development. Also realize that when you harbor anger, you give whatever or whoever angers you the power over your attitude. It's time to take your power back. God wants you at peace. "Get rid of all bitterness, rage and anger, brawling and slander, along with every form of malice. Be kind and compassionate to one another, forgiving each other, just as in Christ God forgave you" (Ephesians 4:31-32).

The following actions will help you implement your decision to let go of anger:

Acknowledge the primary hurt or emotion at the root of your anger.

Become aware of how your anger is manifesting itself (such as surliness or profanity).

Control anger's impact on your body by inhaling deeply and exhaling with an affirmation such as "Thank you, Father" or "I receive Your peace now."

Watch your tone and language in all your communications, not just with the person who has angered you. Request rather than demand. You'll feel more in control, and people will be more inspired to cooperate with you.

Make a decision to forgive. You'll know you have forgiven when you no longer want to see your perpetrator punished. Don't confuse this with the fact that you still feel the hurt. Emotions follow behavior. If you keep reopening the wound by always talking about the offense, it will never heal. Keep doing the right thing. You have a helper, the Holy Spirit.

Talk to a counselor if you believe you need more hands-on enforcement.

Avoid vindictive or negative people who encourage your old behavior.

The Defiant Attitude

■ ■ ■ ■

Rebellious, insubordinate toward those in authority

From Adam and Eve to the insubordinate employee who defies the boss's orders, rebellion is in our nature. However, submission to authority is not optional for the child of God.

> Everyone must submit to governing authorities. For all authority comes from God, and those in positions of authority have been placed there by God. So anyone who rebels against authority is rebelling against what God has instituted, and they will be punished (Romans 13:1-2 NLT).

Since the passage above refers to "all authority," let's start with the family, particularly the husband and wife relationship. I must tread lightly here, but God's requirement is clear.

> For wives, this means submit to your husbands as to the Lord. For a husband is the head of his wife as Christ is the head of the church. He is the Savior of his body, the church. As the church submits to Christ, so you wives should submit to your husbands in everything. For husbands, this means love your wives, just as Christ loved the church. He gave up his life for her to make her holy and clean, washed by the cleansing of God's word (Ephesians 5:22-26 NLT).

Spousal abuse is epidemic in our society, and many wives have become turned off by the concept of submission as harsh husbands, unwise or chauvinistic pastors, and certain counselors cite the Bible's charge only to the wife. This is a gross misapplication of Scripture. A careful reading shows that God's ideal is for wives to submit to their husbands and for husbands to love their wives sacrificially, as Christ loved the church. No husband could use this passage to justify abusing his wife.

If you are a rebellious wife, or wife-to-be, and find the whole notion of submission distasteful, I want to remind you of a few consequences of willful disobedience to this passage:

- A defiant wife robs her husband of his God-given leadership role and may motivate him to default on his responsibilities.

- By her actions a defiant wife can cause resentment, which may show up as coldness and lack of intimacy.

- A defiant wife is embarrassing and damaging to a man's self-esteem and may indeed provoke him to be harsh or abusive.

I am not justifying or condoning any of these potential results. This is merely an admonition to be forewarned. I know a man who has proposed to a woman who was sexually abused by her father and now has a negative attitude toward submission, since her mother's submissiveness allowed the abuse to continue. He is having second thoughts about his proposal, and rightly so, since she rebels against the simplest request he makes—even in the presence of his friends—which he finds humiliating.

Defiance on the job can have dire consequences as well. Whether you were passed over for a promotion, assigned an incompetent boss, or feel that you have been treated unfairly, submission is still the order of the day. In many companies, insubordination is official justification for termination. Except for matters of legality or violation of your personal convictions, there is never a reason to resist your superior's request. Even when you must for legal or moral reasons, watch the tone and spirit in which you refuse to obey.

Note the sensitivity Daniel, the Jewish captive, used in response to the king's order to eat non-kosher food.

> The king assigned them a daily amount of food and wine from the king's table...But Daniel resolved not to defile himself with the royal food and wine, and he asked the chief official for permission not to defile himself this way (Daniel 1:5,8).

What wisdom and finesse! Daniel was not defiant even though he had already decided that under no circumstances was he going to comply with the order. His humble request for a vegetarian diet was granted, and all ended well.

An insubordinate attitude will buy you a one-way ticket to nowhere. (If you happen to manage an insubordinate subordinate, nip his disrespectful behavior in the bud. When insubordination is tolerated, the employee feels emboldened to continue it. Before you know it, you will have lost the respect of the rest of your staff and peers.)

Whether you are a defiant wife, employee, student, teenager, or other, know that God hates rebellion and sees it as sin. Scripture reminds us that "obedience is better than sacrifice, and submission is better than offering the fat of rams. Rebellion is as sinful as witchcraft, and stubbornness as bad as worshiping idols" (1 Samuel 15:22-23 NLT).

As you consider your tendency to be defiant, try to uncover and understand the root cause, which may include one of more of the following:

- painful history of suffering or being victimized
- disrespect for an incompetent superior
- pride because of your superior skills
- unfair treatment from those in authority
- ploy to test the sincerity, care, or concern of an authority figure

Commit today to ridding yourself of the evil of a defiant attitude. Stop and pray about your response when tempted to rebel. Do you want to continue to pay the cost for such an attitude? The choice is yours.

Day 5

Managing Your Sanity

Scheduling Your Day Wisely

■ ■ ■ ■

The LORD makes firm the steps of the one who delights in him.

PSALM 37:23

Each new day presents us with 1440 minutes to use at our discretion. If we don't consciously decide how we will spend them, we will look up and realize they passed us by without our ever starting the tasks we desired to complete. The best approach to this problem is to prepare and follow a wisely prioritized to-do list. I should warn you up front that the list itself can become a source of stress if you include too many tasks. My friend Sandra always cautions me to schedule only two or so "majors" in a day. For example, if I have to take my mother to a doctor's appointment in the afternoon, it may not be a good idea to schedule a two-hour hair appointment or other time-consuming activity that same day. I use an electronic calendar, and I categorize every activity by its importance. Contrary to the thinking of some, every activity is not equally important. You really can put off until tomorrow those insignificant things that would stress you if you were to do them today. If you are not in the habit of developing a to-do list, you may wander aimlessly throughout the day without a sense of focus. Even if you do not have a fancy personal digital assistant (PDA), a simple handwritten list will provide the same sense of accomplishment as you strike off the completed items.

Like me, many of you may be guilty of Star Wars thinking when it comes to scheduling your day: you think everything can be done at light speed. Consequently, you do not build in time for interruptions, lost keys, or for people who move at a snail's pace. This has caused me great stress in the past. I used to rarely plan for extra traffic due to accidents, lane closures, and so forth. Imagine living in Los Angeles with that kind of thinking when at times you can literally read a newspaper on the freeway during rush hour traffic.

Of course, the biggest problem I used to have with my to-do list was that I often forgot to submit it to God. I prepared it the night before and printed it out so I could hit the ground running the next morning. I'm reminded of a phrase in the song "What a Friend We Have in Jesus" that says, "O what peace we often forfeit, O what needless pain we bear, all because we do not carry everything to God in prayer." I was literally giving up my right to peace by not letting God approve my schedule. What I have now learned to do is to prepare the list, hold it up to God, and say, "Lord, this is what I have in mind to do today. Nevertheless, not my will, but Yours be done."

There have been times I have scrapped the entire list and spent most of the day ministering to a friend—and the world never fell apart.

As you plan your schedule, do not plan on doing too many things at the same time. Studies have linked chronic, high-stress multitasking under intense pressure to short-term memory loss. Further, experts have concluded that multitasking actually makes a person more inefficient because it reduces the brain power needed to perform each task.

I know this to be true. I used to pride myself on my ability to juggle several tasks at once. I did not acknowledge the fact that I often had so many piles of paper, opened drawers, and unfinished chaos around me that it almost drove me crazy. Once I was cleaning the house, talking on the phone, and cooking when I heard the smoke detector go off. I had started another project upstairs and had left a skillet of hot oil on the stove. The skillet was in flames and the house was filled with smoke. I was terrified. When the fire department arrived and finally cleared the smoke, I vowed to stop the multitasking—at least while cooking. Darnell has jokingly called me "Fire Marshall Bill" ever since (from the early 1990s television sitcom *In Living Color*).

When working in your office or at home, force yourself to complete a task before starting another one. This will allow you to focus 100 percent of your brain power on the selected task. I have posted a huge note on my desk that says: *Finish one task at a time.* It really helps me to stay focused—and productive.

Finally, if you feel you must be productive during all of your waking minutes, it's time to redefine "productive." Solitude is productive. Taking a mental time-out while waiting in line is productive. Praying for each member of your family while sitting in traffic is productive. Tightening your muscles, memorizing a Scripture (I write them on the backs of my business cards), or praying for all of the souls around you to make it into God's kingdom are all productive pursuits.

Limiting Contact with Stress-Producing People

■ ■ ■ ■

*If it is possible, as far as it depends on
you, live at peace with everyone.*

Romans 12:18

Sometimes it just isn't possible to be at peace with certain people. Acknowledging this reality, the apostle Paul in essence said, "Do all that you can to try and make it happen."

In my day-to-day interactions, I have found it best to evaluate each relationship and to prayerfully determine the extent to which I should invest my time in it. Beyond my spouse, every other relationship is subject to evaluation. Even with him I must express my annoyances and preferences or I will pay the physical and emotional price of sending unresolved anger underground. When I have a close relative who insists on always being argumentative or negative, I refuse to put myself in the position of having to interact with him on a regular basis. Holidays may be frequently enough! The same goes for friends. Those who gossip, criticize others, compete with me, or engage in put-downs will hardly ever find me available—unless the Lord urges me to spend some time with them for the impartation of His Word.

I also try to minimize my contact with people who are constantly distracted by their cell phones or other disruptions to their attention. It drains too much of my time.

We must be careful that we have not become someone's stressor. They say that people who live in glass houses should not throw stones, so I'm going to walk lightly here. I confess that I tend to stress my service providers because I will occasionally need something completed on the same day or right away. I have noticed that one of them has responded by imposing an undisclosed "rush fee."

Even a person's annoying habits can be stress-producing. I have a wonderful brother who worked for more than 30 years for a popular package shipper. The company's daily delivery quota for each driver left no time for dallying. He literally ran to the door of each package recipient. This schedule really took its toll on his health and his habits. To this day he checks his watch every few minutes. We all find his behavior stress-producing and have asked him to stop it.

Another habit that stresses me is for someone to smack their lips when eating. I have prayed for years to be delivered from my irritation with this. I'm still standing in faith. Consequently, if at all possible, I avoid eating with smackers because I feel compelled to address this socially unacceptable behavior. I'll gladly join them for a walk, but dining is out of the question.

We are not commanded to spend time or interact with people who disrupt our peace. The Bible is full of admonitions to avoid people who jeopardize our tranquility. For example, King Solomon said, "Do not make friends with a hot-tempered person, do not associate with one easily angered" (Proverbs 22:24). The apostle Paul warned, "Watch out for those who cause divisions...Keep away from them" (Romans 16:17).

The next time you find yourself in the company of a stress-producing person, ask yourself these questions: Will this situation produce patience in me if I endure it rather than run away? Why does this person's action stress me? Is it because she is mirroring my behavior? Why am I choosing to continue to interact with her?

Knowing Your Sphere of Influence

■ ■ ■ ■

*And which of you by worrying can add one cubit
to his stature? If you then are not able to do the
least, why are you anxious for the rest?*

LUKE 12:25-26 NKJV

"The armies are coming! The armies are coming!" This was the essence
of the message that caused fear to grip King Jehoshaphat's heart. The mes-
senger reported that three nations had joined forces and were coming to
invade his territory. Talk about pressure! His response to this imminent
threat is an example that we can all emulate when faced with situations that
seem to overwhelm us. I call it the Jehoshaphat S.T.R.E.S.S. Model. The
story is related in 2 Chronicles 20.

S—Seek God's guidance: "And Jehoshaphat feared, and set himself to
seek the Lord" (verse 3 NKJV). Many years prior when his father, King
Asa, had faced a threat from formidable enemies, he had responded by
immediately gathering the silver and gold from the temple and from his
palace and using it to bribe one of the invading kings to defect to his side.
That solved the immediate problem—however, not without great consequence. Although the invasion attempt was abandoned, God became
angry at King Asa's reliance on another king to help him defeat his enemies (see 2 Chronicles 16:1-9). God pronounced Asa's punishment for
the rest of his reign: "You have done a foolish thing, and from now on
you will be at war" (2 Chronicles 16:9). He would live with the stress of
always being at war because he had not sought God's counsel first. King
Jehoshaphat was not going to follow the path of his father. His immediate
response was to seek God's guidance.

What about you? Do you stress out trying to figure out a solution to
a situation instead of determining how God would have you handle it?
Think of the last dilemma you faced. Did you rely on the opinion of your
friends or your self-generated ideas, or was your first thought to seek God?

T—Trust what He tells you to do: "You will not have to fight this battle. Take up your positions; stand firm and see the deliverance the LORD
will give you, Judah and Jerusalem! Do not be afraid; do not be discour-
aged. Go out to face them tomorrow, and the LORD will be with you"

(2 Chronicles 20:17). God's way of resolving our issues can often go against our logic. Perhaps that is why we are often reluctant to approach Him in certain matters. Why would God instruct the army of Jehoshaphat, which was obviously no match for three armies, to show up prepared for a battle they were not expected to fight? That made no sense! Nevertheless, God will often tell us to "position" ourselves to deal with a difficult task or problem we feel totally inadequate to confront. Our challenge is to obey and "position" ourselves for victory.

"But," you may ask, "how do I do that?" Let me give you some examples:

- You "position" yourself when you decide to enter college, even though you may not have done well in high school.

- You "position" yourself when you quit your job at God's urging and start that new business, even though there isn't a long list of customers or clients waiting in the wings.

- You "position" yourself when you sit down to write that book you have always wanted to write by showing up at the computer each day—not with a head full of knowledge, but a heart full of faith that God will meet you there with His words.

God's instruction is to position ourselves to succeed. He just wants us to show up so that He can show Himself strong on our behalf.

R—Remember past victories: "Our God, did you not drive out the inhabitants of this land before your people Israel and give it forever to the descendants of Abraham your friend?" (2 Chronicles 20:7). If God has worked a miracle for you or anyone else in the past, He can do it again. Take faith from recalling His great deeds.

E—Exalt God above the problem: "LORD, the God of our ancestors, are you not the God who is in heaven? You rule over all the kingdoms of the nations. Power and might are in your hand, and no one can withstand you" (2 Chronicles 20:6). In his distress, Jehoshaphat asked rhetorical questions that decreed how big his God was compared to the problem. Sometimes it's hard to look beyond the problem when the reality of it is so close. It is like putting a coin over each eye—it can totally blind you to all that is before you. For every stressful situation, we must remember the words of our heavenly Father, "I am the LORD, the God of all mankind. Is anything too hard for me?" (Jeremiah 32:27).

S—Solicit the prayers and support of others: "Jehoshaphat…proclaimed a fast for all Judah. The people of Judah came together to seek help from the LORD; indeed, they came from every town in Judah to seek him" (2 Chronicles 20:3-4). Here was a leader who understood that he was not the Lone Ranger and that he needed the spiritual power that comes with unified fasting and prayer. He did not hesitate to ask for it. Neither should we. This is not asking for opinions, but for intercession that moves the heart of God.

S—Stand on the promises of God: "Early in the morning they left for the Desert of Tekoa. As they set out, Jehoshaphat stood and said, 'Listen to me, Judah and people of Jerusalem! Have faith in the LORD your God and you will be upheld; have faith in his prophets and you will be successful'" (2 Chronicles 20:20). I can never say too much about the power of hiding God's Word in our hearts so that when we need it, we can readily access and stand on it. When we do so, we can say like the psalmist, "Trouble and distress have come upon me, but your commands give me delight" (Psalm 119:143).

Finally, we would do well to recognize that like Jehoshaphat, we all sometimes face situations of varying degrees that are outside of our area of direct influence or control. The truth of the matter is that we really don't control anything anyway—especially situations that relate to other people's behavior. The fact that God may have used us to pray for, counsel with, or otherwise persuade someone to pursue a certain course of action should not lead us to conclude that we can control him. We were just instruments in God's hands. Only God can change a person's mind. I have several friends who constantly complain about how they are tired of trying to get their irresponsible children, husbands, or other relatives on the right track. They have failed to realize that the issues that are within their circle of concern are not always in their circle of direct influence. They need to let go of the stress of trying to achieve what only God can do. Their wisest action would be to continue to intercede for God to change the person or to change them.

Day 6

Bending Without Breaking

The Defensive Attitude

■ ■ ■ ■

Constantly justifying one's actions to avoid criticism

"Sally, you seemed a little harsh with Mary. I think she was embarrassed at being scolded in front of the other teammates."

Gail was struggling to find the right words; she knew how resistant Sally was to feedback. The words were barely out of her mouth before Sally protested.

"Oh no, you don't understand. You see…"

Here we go again, thought Gail. *She always justifies her behavior, no matter how bad it is.* Gail considered herself a close friend, but frankly, she was fed up with Sally's defensive attitude.

Sally stands in sharp contrast to David, the biblical character who rose from shepherd to king of Israel. In instances where he could have justified his ungodly or unwise action, he quickly acknowledged the error of his ways. For example, when fleeing the wrath of King Saul, he sought the help of a certain priest—a decision that ultimately caused Saul to order the death of 85 priests and their families. Devastated but not defensive, David told the surviving son of the slain priest who had assisted him, "I have caused the death of all your father's family" (1 Samuel 22:22 NLT). Can you imagine taking full responsibility for such a tragic consequence? In another instance, when the prophet Nathan confronted David about his adultery with Bathsheba and his attempt to cover up her resulting pregnancy by having her husband killed, David simply said, "I have sinned against the LORD" (2 Samuel 12:13).

Would you have the emotional or spiritual maturity to make such an admission? Or do you have a tendency to always defend your actions for fear of being judged, criticized, alienated, or rejected? Do you often feel attacked when someone offers feedback whether it is positive or negative? How do you respond? Do you retreat in silence? Counter-accuse or blame your "attacker"? Make hostile comments? Become sarcastic?

When one is on the defensive—whether in sports, the armed forces, or in day-to-day relationships—he is attempting to protect something from a real or perceived opponent. I have noticed that people who have a low self-evaluation feel they must protect themselves from the criticism and judgments of others. Of course, we are all prone to being defensive from time to time. However, if you find this has become a pattern in your life, you might be wise to implement the recommendations below.

Listen to yourself and become aware of your tendency to constantly justify your actions.

Guard against defensive body language. For example, crossing your arms when someone is offering input could be your subconscious way of saying, "I'm closed to what you're saying." Keep your body language positive (as in looking pleasant while listening intently).

Counter the anxiety that comes with feeling attacked by breathing deeply and silently praying, "Lord, I receive Your strength now." Combining this physical and spiritual act will help to minimize your emotional response.

If there is indeed a genuine and credible justification for your action, state it in a calm, unemotional manner. (If you are really brave, ask a trusted friend or coworker if you are being defensive. Then refuse to *become* defensive if the response is yes.)

Don't attack your "attacker." Ask her what she would have done in the situation under discussion. Thank her for sharing her insights.

If you are guilty of a bad decision or wrong behavior, try admitting it long before it comes to the light. A simple, "I made a mistake" will do wonders for your relationships and your confidence once you decide not to let your mistakes define you or sabotage the quality of your life.

Interject humor into the situation. ("Boy, am I batting a thousand or what?" "Just shoot me!")

View feedback as a personal growth opportunity and a tool for developing better relationships. Remember: "Those who disregard discipline despise themselves, but the one who heeds correction gains understanding" (Proverbs 15:32).

Adapting to Change

■ ■ ■ ■

Unwillingness to consider alternate ways of doing things

"A flexible person is a happy person," my husband said, mimicking the expression I always use to adjust my attitude when my precious plans go awry. This was his way of letting me know that something had just gone wrong, but that he was putting forth an effort to "go with the flow."

While I haven't "arrived," I have made great strides in overcoming my rigid attitude. I used to put my plans in cement, and woe unto anybody who changed them. I would most likely strike their names off my list for any future interaction. Thank God for deliverance.

Over 20 years ago, the wife of a long-time friend of mine joined him on one of his revival trips to Los Angeles. When her flight arrived, she learned that her luggage had been lost. The revival service would start shortly. I'm sure she had planned to wear a special outfit, but she showed no frustration or disappointment. Her flexibility and peacefulness affected me in a profound way. I decided then that I would make every effort to become a flexible person. In fact, I renew my commitment each time I observe someone at the height of frustration simply because he refuses to be flexible.

Ray is a typical example. His job as a city maintenance worker requires him to share a truck with another man I'll call Jack. Jack tends to get extremely hot and requires the windows in the vehicle to remain down, even when it's chilly outside. Ray often finds the discomfort unbearable and infuriating. He has confronted Jack several times; company management refuses to get involved. When I counseled him recently, I asked, "Why don't you just take a heavier jacket to work? Jack obviously has a medical condition that causes his problem, and there's a limit to the amount of clothing he can peel off." At first, Ray was stuck on the fact that it just "should not be so." When I pointed out that he was experiencing the most emotional turmoil—typical of inflexible people—he realized that he could continue to live in "Shouldville" or he could simply make the necessary changes.

Someone once said, "Blessed are the flexible, for they shall not be bent out of shape." Such was the case with Naaman, the commander of the Syrian army, who was afflicted with leprosy. His wife's maid, a Jewish captive, suggested that he visit the prophet Elisha to seek healing. He had envisioned the healing scenario before he left home. However, when he arrived, Elisha didn't even bother to come out and greet him.

> But Elisha sent a messenger out to him with this message: "Go and wash yourself seven times in the Jordan River. Then your skin will be restored, and you will be healed of your leprosy." But Naaman became angry and stalked away. "I thought he would certainly come out to meet me!" he said. "I expected him to wave his hand over the leprosy and call on the name of the LORD his God and heal me! Aren't the rivers of Damascus, the Abana and the Pharpar, better than any of the rivers of Israel? Why shouldn't I wash in them and be healed?" So Naaman turned and went away in a rage (2 Kings 5:10-12 NLT).

Even in his needy condition, Naaman clung to his rigid attitude. Had it not been for the wise intervention of his servants, who encouraged him to at least try what the prophet had said, he would not have received his healing. Fortunately, he adjusted his attitude, and after his seventh dip in the dirty Jordan River, his leprosy disappeared.

Do you resist change and insist on your expectations? If so, find a quiet place and reflect on the following questions:

- What are the unknowns that I fear about this change or deviation in plans?
- If none of the things I fear could happen, how could this change improve the quality of my life spiritually, relationally, emotionally, financially, or physically?

- Am I willing to risk God's perfect will by resisting a change He is orchestrating? Your inflexibility is an attempt to control an outcome. Many miss God's best because, like Naaman, they have put Him in a box and are looking only inside the box for their answer. Force yourself to look outside the box by being flexible.

- Am I being lazy or complacent and not wanting to invest the necessary time and effort into the change?

Start to embrace a different way of doing something, even simple things, each day (e.g., go a different way to work, sit in a different section at church, interact with a person you don't know). Also, try meditating on these quotes from great men regarding change:

"Every human has four endowments: self-awareness, conscience, independent will and creative imagination. These give us the ultimate human freedom—the power to choose, to respond, to change" (Steven Covey).

"Change is the law of life. And those who look only to the past or present are certain to miss the future" (John Fitzgerald Kennedy).

"The world hates change yet it is the only thing that has brought progress" (Charles Franklin Kettering).

"One cannot manage change. One can only be ahead of it" (Peter F. Drucker).

Being Flexible

■ ■ ■ ■

The wisdom that comes from heaven is…
peace loving, considerate, submissive.

JAMES 3:17

Flexible people are happy people. They experience a lot less stress than rigid types who insist on things always being done according to policy or exactly the way they have decided they should be done. One of the reasons that inflexibility is so stressful is that we have to achieve our goals and purposes through thinking humans who often have their own bright ideas. If you are not the type who is receptive to new ways of doing things because you view them as a personal rejection of your own ideas, run to the altar and get healing. Otherwise, you will find yourself in a constant state of frustration and stress.

When I worked as a corporate manager with a large staff that included women with children, I had to come to grips with the fact that "life happens" and that there would be many times when they would have to take babies to the doctor, meet with teachers, and participate in a host of other activities that interfered with my planned staff meetings or the work flow. Other employees needed to have their hours adjusted from time to time to meet family and personal demands. At first I was frustrated by all of their requests. While I always allowed them the time off, I inwardly thought, *That's a personal problem that should be worked out away from work.* However, my husband, also a corporate manager who has managed a staff that included mothers, adult children of dependent parents, single parents, and others, convinced me to come into the real world where "life happens" and to develop a new mindset about these realities.

Several years ago corporations realized that if they did not practice flexibility in employee work hours and even their location, they were in danger of demoralizing or losing employees who were key to their bottom line. Today they offer flextime, telecommuting, and a host of other conveniences designed to make work a win-win proposition.

Jesus was a great model of flexibility—much to the dismay of the Pharisees, the Jewish religious sect who insisted on strict adherence to the law. Once He healed a blind man on the Sabbath day. To the Pharisees, this constituted work. "Some of the Pharisees said, 'This man is not from God, for he does not keep the Sabbath'" (John 9:16). He also allowed His disciples to pluck grains from heads of wheat to eat on the Sabbath. Jesus explained His occasional easing of the "policy" this way: "Then he said to them, 'The Sabbath was made for man, not man for the Sabbath'" (Mark 2:27). Can you imagine the stress level of the Pharisees as they tried to enforce every jot and tittle of the law?

How flexible are you? Are you so specific at home that your family stays on edge for fear of violating one of your endless preferences? Must the towels be folded only a certain way? If plans need to be changed due to unforeseeable circumstances, does it send you into a tailspin, or do you stop and consider that God may have a different plan for the day?

If you want to become more flexible, don't try to justify your behavior by hiding under the cloak of excellence. Yes, you'd like to see things done in the best manner possible; however, seek to recognize the times when your behavior leaves the realm of being excellent and begins to border on being an inflexible perfectionist who not only creates stress for yourself, but for others as well.

There is a saying that some people's minds are like concrete, thoroughly mixed up and permanently set. Don't let this be your testimony. Relax. Bend a little. Try going with the flow. Release the stress of inflexibility.

Day 7

Leaving the Past

Overcoming Guilt

■ ■ ■ ■

*If our hearts do not condemn us, we
have confidence before God.*

1 John 3:21

We all sin. When we do so, we either respond by asking for God's forgiveness and going forward believing we will not have a repeat performance, or we get stuck in guilt—always being remorsefully reminded that we have done something wrong. Guilt can cause a great deal of anxiety and insecurity. King Saul's jealousy caused him to seek David's life after David killed Goliath the giant. Saul feared David would take his place as king (1 Samuel 18:8). Saul's insecurity was well-founded. God had already sent word that because of Saul's disobedience, the kingdom was going to be torn from him and given to another.

Many times when we know we have been disobedient or remiss in our responsibilities, we develop anxiety about possible consequences. For instance, many men and women are plagued with jealousy because of their own infidelity or prior indiscretions. They live in great fear that one day they will reap what they have sown. Some have even resorted to verbal and physical abuse of their partner in order to ward off what they feel will be the inevitable. Take the story of someone whom we will call Sarah.

Sarah had an affair with a married man many years ago and now lives with the nagging fear that her husband will one day violate their marriage vows. She is suspicious of most of the women who interact with him. Her insecurity has not gone unnoticed by friends and acquaintances. Further, because Sarah violated God's law as well as her own sense of morality, she is anxious about the punishment she feels she deserves. She confided in me that this keeps her in a state of anxiety and insecurity. How can Sarah break free of her dilemma? She needs to ask for and accept God's forgiveness. This sounds simple, but we all know that it is not easy.

It takes faith to accept God's forgiveness and to release ourselves from guilt and condemnation. When we repent, we must *believe* His promise: "Their sins and lawless acts I will remember no more" (Hebrews 10:17). God doesn't remember confessed sin, so we need to stop rehearsing it. God does not want to hear about it ever again. Paul said, "When sins have been forgiven, there is no need to offer any more sacrifices" (verse 18 NLT). Once is enough. There is no need to repent after the first time. To do so is to offer another sacrifice. Too many people sacrifice the rest of their lives on the altar of remorse over a single transgression. Years ago the phrase "That's dead" was popular among the young and hip. What they meant by it was that the issue or situation was of no more importance or consequence. When God forgives you and the devil comes back to remind you of your past transgression, respond with a shout, "That's dead!"

It is time for Sarah to stop looking through the rearview mirror as she drives down the road of life. She will discover new horizons, emotional freedom, and a stronger relationship with her husband when she focuses on the broad windshield of the future. And no, it is not absolutely necessary for her to confess her prior indiscretion to her husband. Her decision to do so must be anchored in prayer with thoughtful consideration of his level of spiritual and emotional maturity to handle such truth. Otherwise, her confession could cause him to begin to distrust her and thus create a new set of problems.

Many years ago I worked as a vice president in an entertainment conglomerate. The company was preparing to be acquired by another entity. I was devastated to learn that the subsidiary where I was employed would be shut down within the following year as part of the corporate restructuring. I held a plum position that came with a tastefully decorated office—and a very nice compensation package so typical of the entertainment industry. I was certainly not looking forward to a job search.

The salaries in the entertainment industry in general tended to be much higher at that time than other industries. I knew it would be difficult to find a new position with similar benefits, and so I started to become a little anxious. The first thing my husband asked me when I told him that my subsidiary would be shut down was, "Is there any sin in your life?" (Imagine!) I assured him I was current regarding confession of sin. I try to make it a habit to keep the door of repentance swinging so that my channel to God stays clear. He then assured me that we could relax and believe God for His provision.

With confidence in God's promise to multiply the seeds we had planted not only in our church, but also in the lives of others, and with confidence that we had walked in obedience and integrity with our finances, I released all anxiety—that is, until about 30 days before the designated shutdown date. I had not received a single job offer—primarily due to the fact that I had only told a few acquaintances of my plight and had not sent out a single résumé. One Saturday Darnell and I were riding in the car and I exclaimed in frustration, "Lord, if You let me down, I'm going to tell everybody!" Imagine, threatening to ruin God's reputation. Appalled at my statement, Darnell said, "God, that is her side of the car. Please don't strike me dead." A few weeks later, a Fortune 500 company, through an executive recruiter, offered me a high-level position at a 20 percent raise! The job was created and the responsibilities defined *after* I had been on board several weeks with very little to do. God had done it again!

We need to make every effort to line our lives up with God's requirements. When we do so, it has a big impact on our sense of security. "The fruit of that righteousness will be peace; its effect will be quietness and confidence forever" (Isaiah 32:17).

Do you have an unconfessed sin that is keeping you from walking in total confidence? Repent now and accept God's forgiveness.

Are you still repenting over a sin you committed long ago? Dare you rest now that you know God doesn't even remember it?

The Victim Attitude

■ ■ ■ ■

Continual focus on personal helplessness and
powerlessness due to past misfortunes

The afflicted man who had lain for many years at the pool called Bethesda in Jerusalem had every reason to feel hopeless. He had suffered from his condition for 38 long years. A number of disabled people would gather at this pool because on certain occasions an angel of the Lord would come down and stir the water, and the first person to enter the water after the stirring would be healed. Naturally, there was stiff competition from the many infirm people at the pool. Because of his limited mobility, this man had yet to win first place and had become a fixture by the pool. But that was about to change.

> When Jesus saw him lying there and learned that he had been in this condition for a long time, he asked him, "Do you want to get well?" "Sir," the invalid replied, "I have no one to help me into the pool when the water is stirred. While I am trying to get in, someone else goes down ahead of me" (John 5:6-7).

Good grief! Why didn't he just say, "Yes, I want to be healed"? Why did he explain the woes of his past instead? He obviously held on to a ray of hope or he would have resigned all efforts and returned home. Could it be that he had begun to enjoy being the guest of honor at his own pity party? This man was a genuine victim. In addition to his paralysis, he suffered the great tragedy of not having a loyal friend or family member to assist him in his effort to be made whole. Scripture says, "A friend loves at all times, and a brother is born for a time of adversity" (Proverbs 17:17). Why was his support system conspicuously absent? I don't know the answers to these questions, but he serves as a great reminder that we should be careful to nurture our relationships.

Now this chapter is not directed toward victims of recent crimes or other tragic events but rather to those who may have been victimized in the past (e.g., spousal or parental abandonment, sexual or verbal abuse, discrimination) and have not been able to move forward. Their self-pity has become their ticket to getting the attention they desire. My message is clear: You always have the option of a different response.

Take Job, for instance. He was a good man, "blameless and upright; he feared God and shunned evil" (Job 1:1). He could have easily felt victimized by God, who allowed Satan to take away his children, his health, and his wealth in short order. Yet, "In all this, Job did not sin by charging God with wrongdoing" (Job 1:22). What a model!

Whether the beef is with God or a human being, the victim is stuck in an unresolved offense and refuses to let the emotional wound heal. French philosopher Voltaire cautioned, "The longer we dwell on our misfortunes, the greater is their power to harm us." A person with a victim's mindset stays on high alert for continued offenses by others to validate and reinforce her victimhood.

What about you? Do you want to be made well? If you are willing to admit to having this attitude, let's look at some ways that you can begin to overcome it.

Get a new perspective on the hurtful offenses of the past. Since "in all things God works for the good of those who love him, who have been called according to his purpose" (Romans 8:28), ask God to show you what "good" can come out of your pain. When Ann, a black college student, faced extreme discrimination at the hands of her English professor, she decided she would hone her writing and communication skills to perfection. She later became a bestselling author. Today, she says she's grateful for the incident and how it shaped her destiny.

Decide to forgive all the people who have victimized you. Consider that some people on your list may only be *perceived* victimizers since you have viewed everyone through your "victim's lens." For now, forget about *feeling* differently toward them. Forgiveness is a decision to release a relational debt; it is not an emotion.

Solicit the support of others you trust. Give them permission to let you know when your victim attitude is rearing up when they observe you sabotaging a relationship because of your past.

Stop giving substance and reinforcement to a victim mentality. Refuse to discuss slights or other perceived acts of victimization. "The boss doesn't like me." "My wife never supports my goals." "Everybody's raise is higher than mine." "Not one of my employees acknowledged my birthday."

Cast down thoughts of defeat, rejection, and alienation. Let your smile, your generosity, and your genuine concern for others draw people to you. Take responsibility for the rest of your life by taking decisive action. Jesus told our friend from the pool of Bethesda, "Get up! Pick up your mat and walk" (John 5:8). Do something. Get started on your future. No more excuses!

Dealing with Disappointments

■ ■ ■ ■

Many are the plans in a person's heart, but it is the LORD's purpose that prevails.

PROVERBS 19:21

During my senior year of college, I became engaged to a young man whom I'll call Tom. I had visions of us both climbing the corporate ladder and living happily ever after. He was a rising star in a Fortune 500 corporation, handsome, and a Christian. However, like Naaman the leper in 2 Kings 5, he had a proverbial spot: He was extremely jealous. He did not even want my own mother to buy me a gift. At first I found his devotion to me endearing. Then I began to see that he had taken it to the extreme because of his insecurity. Things came to a head when I visited my mother in Los Angeles during my last summer of college. During my stay, I also paid a visit to his uncle, who turned out to be very flirtatious. When he made a pass at me, I rebuffed him. To retaliate, he called my fiancé and accused me of having an affair with someone. Tom believed every word—as a typical insecure person would. He was so upset that he broke off our relationship. I felt as though the end of the world had come.

After graduation, I immediately moved to Los Angeles. I prayed to be reconciled with Tom for almost a year. I did everything I had heard faith ministers teach. I claimed Tom as my husband. I reclaimed him daily. God said no, but I wasn't having it. I was convinced that Satan was holding up my blessing. I kept petitioning God. "Doesn't Your Word say that You will give me the desires of my heart? Is that deal still on? And what about Mark 11:24? Doesn't it say that whatever I ask for, if I believe that I'll receive it, I'll have it?" God seemed to dig His heels in and kept saying no.

I finally accepted the fact that it just wasn't going to happen and moved on with my life. About seven years later, I met my husband, Darnell, who is one of the most secure men on the planet. I thank God to this day that He did not answer my prayer to be reunited with Tom. I would have been miserable! It was through this emotional storm and many others since then that I have learned the truth of Romans 8:28: "And we know that in all things God works for the good of those who love him, who have been called according to his purpose."

I have seen many women forge ahead to solidify a relationship in which God had thrown up a zillion red flags—and they rationalized away each one. The disappointment that sets in after the marriage is sure to generate a great deal of stress.

I have concluded that the first three letters of the word disappointment are an acronym for *Divinely Initiated Stop*. Since disappointment is in essence the death of a plan, our best response is to grieve it and move on. Now, I don't mean to make this sound simplistic, but trying to work outside of God's will is like trying to dig your way through a brick wall with a fork. Rather than digging your way out of prison, you will dig yourself into one when you insist on getting what you want. It can be debilitating and stress-producing to make attempt after attempt to get the desired thing to come to fruition. Each day I am practicing not allowing myself to get stuck in a disappointment ditch for very long. "The LORD of Heaven's Armies has spoken—who can change his plans? When his hand is raised, who can stop him?" (Isaiah 14:27 NLT).

Do you really want to pursue a plan God has not ordained? Can you trust Him enough to know what is best for you? Don't stress out over what should have been. If God had ordained it, it would have happened. If He has not, run the other way.

Day 8

Exiting the Fast Lane

The Impatient Attitude

■ ■ ■ ■

Irritation with anything that causes delay

"So what's the bottom line?" Jill wanted to shout at the woman who was giving the support group the long version of her current dilemma. It was getting late, and five members were still waiting for their turn to share the issues they had faced during the week.

As a trained counselor, Jill knew she had to resist the urge to show her impatience. Sure she was high-strung and impatient in general, but she'd recently had an "aha" moment during a Bible study at church. She had finally gotten it: patience is a *fruit* of the Holy Spirit. It wasn't something that she could achieve through a New Year's resolution or by counting to ten; it could be *produced* in her only by the Spirit of God—with her cooperation.

Perhaps you, along with me, share Jill's challenge in this area. In my quest to understand the root cause of my tendency to become impatient with others, I reminded myself that we are all a product of a fast-paced, instant-gratification society where we have become accustomed to instant communication (phone, texting, instant messaging), instant food, instant credit, instant news, high-speed Internet, and a host of other "now" conveniences that cause us to become annoyed at waiting for *anything*. Our impatience has far-reaching consequences since it affects us physically, emotionally, and relationally. We need a major shift in our expectations regarding how fast we should move or the pace at which we expect others to do so.

I've decided, for starters, to take control over the physical impact of impatience. The minute I feel the anxiety and the corresponding (very harmful) adrenaline rush, I acknowledge this insidious enemy and take full responsibility for its cause and my response.

For example, sometimes I feel impatience rear its ugly head when I'm helping my mom and her elderly friends get into my vehicle. Often my mind is focused on the rest of the day's tasks and the limited time that I have to complete them. As these women move at a snail's pace, I have learned to call upon God for His help, breathe deeply, lower my expectation, and make a mental note to prioritize the day differently next time. I also thank God that they are alive and that I have the opportunity to serve them. I also acknowledge when my poor planning and ineffective time management have played a role in organizing the day.

I try to use a similar strategy in every "waiting" situation I encounter. Why should I become perturbed with the grocery checker, the bank teller, or the slow driver because she doesn't move at warp speed? Why not prepare to wait by keeping a book or magazine (or CD in the car) handy? Further, I also believe delays are often part of divine protection. I heard stories of people who escaped the destruction of the September 11 terrorist attack on the World Trade Center simply because they were delayed in getting to work for various reasons. I'm sure most were perturbed with the delay at the time it occurred.

Impatience affects us emotionally since we feel angry and exasperated when things do not go the way we think they should. Our ability to endure delays without emotional interference will preserve our joy and keep us at peace.

Impatience hurts our relationships in that it causes us to relate to others in a nonbeneficial, noncompassionate manner. Think about how you feel when even a stranger is short-tempered with you. Depending on your spiritual maturity, you either want to retaliate or run from his presence. If this person is significant to you and you value his perception of you, his impatience can rob you of your confidence and make you feel devalued. Remember this when you are tempted to express your impatience even in the form of a deep sigh.

Once when I managed an extremely incompetent staff member in whom I had invested endless hours in training and development, I found myself sighing in his presence to express my disappointment with his performance. What I did not realize at the time was that, rather than motivating him, my response decreased his effectiveness even more. His anxiety increased, causing his emotions to sabotage his ability to think clearly.

Overcoming impatience begins with an awareness of its presence, a commitment to allow the Holy Spirit to produce patience in you, and a decision to stay in the present moment rather than obsessing about what must happen next or later.

Taking a Time-Out

■ ■ ■ ■

*Jesus said, "Let's go off by ourselves to a
quiet place and rest awhile."*

MARK 6:31

God commanded the observance of the Sabbath day for good reason: for man to rest from his labors. If He, being supernatural, felt that He should rest after six days of creation activity, how much more should we? Many people today are going nonstop the way ants prepare for the winter—with rarely a break.

Jesus was a big proponent of resting. Once He sent His disciples on an evangelistic tour, and they came back bursting with excitement about all of the wonderful miracles they had performed. He responded in a manner that we would find odd. You would think that He would have encouraged them to keep up the momentum. Not so. "Then Jesus said, 'Let's go off by ourselves to a quiet place and rest awhile.' He said this because there were so many people coming and going that Jesus and his apostles didn't even have time to eat. So they left by boat for a quiet place, where they could be alone" (Mark 6:31-32). Does this sound like your average day in which things are so busy you rarely get a chance to take a break? Jesus was quite concerned that His disciples had no leisure. What did He know that we seem to keep missing? He never rushed around, never seemed to be stressed or controlled by the crowds, and kept His priorities straight.

Jesus knew the importance rest and relaxation played in His disciples' continued effectiveness, so He insisted upon it.

In the past I have had to repent for how I abused my body by not taking regular breaks throughout the day. Why, I even bragged that I could work eight to ten hours straight without taking any break at all. I wore it like a badge of honor. I did not know then that I was stressing my joints and putting undue strain on my back. Short breaks are essential in managing stress. Longer breaks are equally critical. If your dream of a great getaway keeps getting pushed to the back burner, maybe it's time to revisit your approach to it. Why not experience it in smaller doses? Search your local newspaper or the Internet for low-cost specials. Darnell and I have committed to a weekend getaway at least once a quarter. Further, as we discussed ways for controlling our schedules, we also decided that we would leave one Saturday of each month open to do whatever we like—without a single outside obligation. We have vowed to guard this time by putting notes on our calendars that say "Do Not Book." Time-outs won't happen without a firm resolve and careful planning. You have to begin to deem your leisure time as important as any other commitment.

If you are married, you will not be doomed if you occasionally plan a short time away from your spouse. As I write this, I am on a five-day getaway in Palm Springs, California—alone. The solitude, time alone with God, and leisurely pace have really rejuvenated my mind and my spirit. Notwithstanding, it is essential that couples spend time away together to reconnect and to rekindle the fire. It is important that each spouse has a clear understanding of what to expect on the vacation so that the vacation itself doesn't become a source of stress and failed expectations. After a few disappointing trips to the snow, Darnell finally concluded that I am not the type that will be skiing down mountains or engaging in any other dangerous sports. We now agree in advance that he will probably play a few rounds of golf, will have a limited desire to shop, and will want to read a novel he has been saving for vacation. However, since we are on vacation *together*, we also agree on what activities we can enjoy as a couple, such as tandem bike riding, movies, and, of course, dinner. We even call "time-out" on certain conversations so that we can really vacate the stressors that make time away so essential.

Many pastors' wives have confided in me that their vacations are usually no fun (if they occur at all) because the pastors are constantly on the phone and never disconnect from the congregation. I wonder what Jesus would say about that!

If you are single and do not want to vacation alone, consider taking a really fun friend with you. It will surely be less expensive; however, don't let the cost be the deciding factor.

Remember that a getaway is supposed to de-stress you. It is a time of rest and relaxation for your physical and mental health, so make it a good one.

Slowing Your Pace

■ ■ ■ ■

You will not leave in a hurry, running for your lives. For the LORD will go ahead of you; yes, the God of Israel will protect you from behind.

ISAIAH 52:12

God was about to orchestrate the freedom of the Israelites who found themselves once again in bondage to an enemy nation. He cautioned them not to stress out about their deliverance by hurrying around and running for their lives. He wanted them to settle down in the knowledge that He had their backs and was going to lead them out every step of the way without chaos.

One of the most common maladies of this century is "Hurry Sickness." You can identify its sufferers everywhere you go. They dart in and out of lanes in gridlocked traffic; they try to be the first ones off the plane, even though they will still have to wait an eternity at baggage claim; they honk at you if you don't take off like a jackrabbit when the traffic signal turns green; they drum their fingers against whatever they can find when they have to wait; they punch the elevator button repeatedly to make the elevator come faster; they click their writing pens to the point of making those around them want to go berserk. These people remind me of hummingbirds. These tiny birds can fly forward and also hover in midair going nowhere. Their tiny wings can move up to 75 times each second! The average life span of a hummingbird is only three years. I cannot help but compare them to the eagle. Eagles live an average of 30 years. Rather than excessive wing flapping, they soar. They can stay aloft for hours flowing with the wind currents. Eagles can be spotted at altitudes of 10,000 feet. When we stop rushing and start soaring with the wind of the Holy Spirit, like the eagle, we will last a lot longer and go much higher than we ever dreamed.

I realized how my "hurry habit" was affecting my family one day when I called from an out of town trip to speak to my five-year-old niece. When my brother called her to the phone, I heard him say, "Hurry! It's Auntie Deborah." The truth of the matter was that I was *not* in a hurry and had set time aside to talk to her for as long as she liked. However, I had developed a reputation for scheduling every moment of the day and for only having a limited time for every activity. Most people assumed that when I called, they needed to expedite the conversation. I was really taken aback because I knew I had earned this reputation. I did indeed have a hard time dealing with people who talked or moved slowly. When I interacted with them, I tried to speed them up by talking or moving faster—hoping they would emulate my behavior. I would deliberately answer my phone at home and at work with a "hello" that sounded as though I were rushing to put out a fire. Getting the hint, most callers would go into high gear to get to the point. My husband told me to stop answering the phone if I did not have time to talk. He said it was a put off to others. A few close friends confirmed his assessment.

Have you considered the possibility that your pace may be stressing others? If you are the impatient type that tends to move faster than most, there is a good chance you cause others to interact with you at a speed outside their comfort zone. For them, this spells stress. Now, in your defense, I submit that your job may have played a role in your developing this behavior. If you find that you always seem to be in a hurry mode and you have done everything within your power to fix the situation, such as proper staffing, effective delegation, and good time management, then it may be time to seek God's will regarding a change of employment. Is it really worth your life? Isn't a quality life at the core of why you work?

Know that every time you get into a hurry mode you send a "state of emergency" signal to your body. It responds by releasing the stress hormones adrenaline and cortisol that prepare you to deal with danger. The body cannot distinguish between physical danger, the danger of losing your job, or any other form of pressure being brought to bear. It only knows that action has to be taken and that it must energize you to deal with it. Now, this is a good thing if you are indeed physically threatened, but to live with your body always on high alert is like fighting a 15-round nonstop boxing match. You will eventually pay the price in the form of heart disease, high cholesterol, ulcers, forgetfulness, and a host of other conditions.

What is the cure for the hurry habit? It's as simple as A-B-C: Awareness, Belief, and Change. Become *aware* of your constant high-gear mode and what role you play in each instance of your hurrying. Ask yourself, "How could I have avoided this?" *Believe* that the Holy Spirit can and will give you the victory if you ask Him. *Change* your behavior. Consciously start to slow down. Talk slower. Move slower. Heed the adage that "haste makes waste." Haste causes duplication of work, accidents, and other perils that result in more lost time.

My incidents of "haste makes waste" are legion. They have ranged from finding the cordless phone receiver in the refrigerator to running over my laptop computer that I thought I had put in the trunk of my car. Further, I used to talk so fast that in my conversations with others, they constantly asked me to repeat what I had said. I found this so frustrating and would silently scold them by thinking, *Just listen faster, Snail!* I enrolled in a speech class designed to cure my problem. The instructor required me to read a short passage of text in a very deliberate manner and to slowly pronounce each syllable of each word. The selection had to be stretched for a minimum number of minutes. If I finished it too quickly, I had to repeat it. It helped me tremendously. This is a good exercise to practice at home if you are a speed talker. You could start by reading a page of material at your regular pace. Note how much time it required. Then, try taking twice as long reading the same material. I found it helpful to tape my session with a small recorder. Nevertheless, I frequently revert to my speed-talking ways when I get excited. Whenever I speak in public, I usually assign someone the task of signaling me if my speech has gone into warp speed.

Deciding to move at a slower pace will definitely improve the quality of your life. Don't try to do it alone. God wants to help you. "Be still, and know that I am God" (Psalm 46:10).

Day 9

Good Enough

Imagining Inadequacy

■ ■ ■ ■

Not that we are competent in ourselves to claim anything
for ourselves, but our competence comes from God.

2 CORINTHIANS 3:5

Elihu seems to have appeared at Job's house out of nowhere. There is no mention of him during the first 31 chapters of the book of Job. Rather, we see Job's three finger-pointing, so-called friends, accuse him of causing his own suffering. Having read the story, we know that Satan was behind Job's physical, emotional, and financial afflictions. In chapter 32 of this saga, when the three miserable comforters ceased their lengthy discourses, Elihu decided to speak. Evidently, he had been present all along—but had kept silent. He listened with great patience as Eliphaz, Bildad, and Zophar made their extensive arguments. When Elihu finally spoke, he explained why he had kept silent: "I am young in years, and you are old; that is why I was fearful, not daring to tell you what I know. I thought, 'Age should speak; advanced years should teach wisdom'" (Job 32:6-7).

Elihu was intimidated by the age and experience of Job's friends and assumed they were wiser than he. His imagined inadequacy had silenced him. In his eyes, he was not qualified to express an opinion on the cause of Job's suffering. Why, he couldn't even hold a candle to these icons of wisdom. Therefore, he relegated himself to the listening corner. However, after hearing their long and meaningless discourses, he realized that their perspective on Job's problem was not superior to his. Feeling emboldened, Elihu suddenly knew that he, too, had some ideas that were worth putting on the table. He continued: "But it is the spirit in a person, the breath of the Almighty, that gives them understanding. It is not only the old who are wise, not only the aged who understand what is right. Therefore, I say: Listen to me; I too will tell you what I know" (Job 32:8-10). He spoke nonstop for six chapters. He no longer saw himself as the loser in the game of comparison.

We must be careful to monitor what we allow to occupy our minds lest it becomes our reality. Can you recall a time when you felt so inadequate that you kept quiet and refused to speak up, even though you had a worthwhile thought or idea? As did Elihu, you must realize that it is not your ability, your knowledge, or your experience that determines your success. The "secret to success" is total dependence on the enabling power of the Holy Spirit. The apostle Paul so aptly stated, "By the grace of God I am what I am" (1 Corinthians 15:10 NKJV). Once you become fully persuaded of this fact, you will begin to take on new levels of risk or responsibility without fear of failure. You will have finally understood that God never gives a person a responsibility without giving him the ability to respond. Why not stop, look in the mirror right now, and say to yourself, "When God gives me a responsibility, He gives me the ability to respond!"

Several men in the Bible felt an overwhelming sense of inadequacy when God gave them an assignment that would later cause them to become known as great men. Let's look at a couple of them. Observe their confessed insecurities and the accomplishments they made when enabled by the grace of God.

When God told Gideon to lead the Israelites in the battle against the powerful Midianites, he cited his inadequacy for the job because of certain insecurities he had. "'Pardon me, my lord,' Gideon replied, 'but how can I save Israel? My clan is the weakest in Manasseh, and I am the least in my family.' The LORD answered, 'I will be with you, and you will strike down all the Midianites, leaving none alive'" (Judges 6:15-16). Gideon went to battle and conquered an army of 135,000 with only 300 soldiers—plus God. That was a ratio of 450 to 1! It takes the presence of omnipotence to achieve those results with such limited resources.

I am totally convinced that there are no great men or women, but rather ordinary people who have obeyed God's command to do the extraordinary. God delights in exalting those who are inadequate in their own sight. So the next time Satan reminds you that you are inadequate, agree with him. "You are correct! I am indeed inadequate. However, I am connected to the Supreme Being, who is all-powerful, all-knowing, and always present. Through Him, I can do all things!"

The only real prerequisite for success is obedience. You must exercise faith and show up for the job. Are you ready to be the vessel through whom God can demonstrate His power? If so, He is looking for you. "For the eyes of the LORD run to and fro throughout the whole earth, to show Himself strong on behalf of those whose heart is loyal to Him" (2 Chronicles 16:9 NKJV).

What excuse have you made for not pursuing a certain task? Do you really think that the excuse is above God's ability to overcome?

Personal Devaluation

■ ■ ■ ■

She perceives that her merchandise is good.

PROVERBS 31:18 NKJV

Despite her perfect surroundings in the Garden of Eden, Eve believed the serpent's lie that she had inadequate knowledge and needed to eat the forbidden fruit to improve her lot.

Mental health professionals and life coaches, as well as popular clergy, have offered various solutions to the dilemma of low self-evaluation—only to find that it is still an unrelenting emotional plague. Our perception of personal inadequacy persists because we do not fully grasp the value or worth our Creator has embedded in us.

In many ways, the worth of a person can be compared to the value of money. When a government establishes its currency, the exchange value on the face of it is permanent—no matter how it appears physically. Assume, for example, that you have a $100 bill that is worn, torn, and otherwise disfigured. The fact that it is no longer new and crisp does not diminish its value. No matter how it looks, its value remains unchanged simply because it was established by its maker. It will always be worth $100 and can be used to obtain whatever any $100 bill normally purchases. Imagine if you were shopping and presented a merchant with a motley $100 bill to pay for your goods or service. If he were to respond with, "Sorry, I can't give you full value because your currency is battered and torn," you would conclude that the merchant was nuts.

Further, there is a serial number on every single bill of currency that gives it a unique identity. Likewise, God created each of us with an exclusive identity and value. We honor Him when we embrace our uniqueness.

The nameless superwoman described in Proverbs 31:10-31 has been the subject of many sermons. In this narrative, King Lemuel recites the advice his mother gave him regarding the character traits and behavior patterns that he should look for in the woman he planned to marry. I find verse 18 particularly encouraging for those who battle insecurity: "She perceives that her merchandise is good" (NKJV). Let's look at five liberating truths found in this simple phrase.

1. *She* perceives that her merchandise is good. She is not one who comes to the table looking for validation or approval of her wares. When one is insecure and does not personally value what she brings to the table, others may be able to minimize it or convince her that it does not rate. This woman, like all humans, desires acceptance and validation, but she will not seek it or find herself debilitated if she does not get it.

2. She *perceives* that her merchandise is good. To perceive is to sense, know, or understand inwardly. She understands what she brings to the table and she inwardly values it. She will not doubt the value of its worth; neither will she find it necessary to brag about the quality of her merchandise. The ideal woman will not have her nose turned up in pride, but neither will her eyes be cast down with false humility. She simply has a balanced view of her wares. Notice that she does not pretend that her merchandise is good, for it is hypocritical and difficult to attempt to fake confidence. The facade will soon become evident to the discerning person. No, Mrs. Proverbs 31 simply perceives the worth of her wares. Beware. Even if you have the utmost confidence, someone may still attempt to minimize your worth and say that what you bring is of little or no value—but their opinion will not faze you when you are fully persuaded on the inside, when you perceive your value.

3. She perceives that *her* merchandise is good. Here is a woman who is not intimidated by or unduly concerned about the goods of the other merchants. Consequently, she doesn't spend her energies comparing or competing. Her merchandise speaks for itself. As a Christian, competing

for anything in life outside of the area of sports is as pointless as trying to outrun another car on the freeway. Both drivers have a different destination. Why should you compete with another person for your destiny when God has already ordained it? I find great encouragement in the psalmist's reminder, "All the days ordained for me were written in your book before one of them came to be" (Psalm 139:16).

4. She perceives that her *merchandise* is good. This woman has current confidence. She is not stuck in the past, thinking about the good merchandise she used to have. Neither is she postponing the pursuit of her goals until her merchandise is perfect. She simply steps out in faith, having done the best she could. Her merchandise is good today; tomorrow is in God's hands. Anxiety has no place in her life.

5. This mentally and morally strong woman perceives that her merchandise is *good*. She embraces and values what she brings to the marketplace. She refuses to allow man, media, or merchants to define or set the standard for her merchandise. You see, your merchandise is whatever you offer to the world. It could simply be a positive attitude, integrity, confidentiality, loyalty, or any other intangible quality. And, although society may not set a great store by it or grant you special recognition because of it, you must perceive within yourself, as part of your personal, biblically based value system, that your merchandise is good.

Further, there really is no need to feel inadequate around anybody when you have an intimate relationship with the One who created everybody. Someone once said, "He who kneels before God can stand before anyone."

What merchandise do you bring to the table? Do you really perceive that it is good?

The Knowledge Deficit

■ ■ ■ ■

My people are destroyed from lack of knowledge.

HOSEA 4:6

People will go to great lengths to keep from appearing unknowledgeable. You may have had the experience of talking to someone and discerning from the look in his eyes that he did not comprehend the subject matter, but rather than saying so, he simply nodded. Well, I confess that I have done the same thing a time or so in my life. God forbid that I should have appeared ignorant! Now that I have come to grips with the truth that I'll never know everything, I try to enhance the self-esteem of others by allowing them to shine while I learn. I love picking people's brains about their life experiences.

If "knowledge is power," then we can conclude that "lack of knowledge is powerlessness." What you don't know will hurt you. Those with inadequate knowledge will be powerless to compete for top wages and promotions. Such powerlessness only deepens one's sense of insecurity.

Basic survival skills today—and even more so in the future—will require adequate knowledge beyond technical know-how. Let's face it. People most often judge your intelligence, education, and ability to succeed by how well you speak and the extent of your vocabulary. Numerous studies have shown that there is a direct correlation between vocabulary and income levels.

During my career in corporate America, I witnessed individuals with less practical experience gain the edge over their coworkers because of their strong command of the English language. Developing good verbal and written communication skills, whether through formal classes or self-study, is one of the greatest confidence-building endeavors one could undertake. It enhances a person's sense of security to know that he can hold his own in any group and communicate effectively without searching for words. Gaining skills in this area can be done easily and conveniently through Internet sites, word-a-day calendars, tapes, and books.

To walk in confidence is to walk with faith. In fact, the prefix "con" means "with" and the root "fid" means "faith or trust." How emotionally liberating it is to know that we can walk with the faith and conviction that we are enabled by God who knows everything, is all-powerful, and is always present.

Caution! Beware of information overload. It is impossible to keep up with all of the news and developments on a worldwide or even local basis. Everyone has to find his own comfort zone as to how much information he wants to acquire. I have made a conscious decision to be knowledgeable only in the areas that relate to my current life focus or to specific matters within my circle of concern. Beyond that, I have resorted to reading the "Highlights" and "Opinion" sections of the newspaper and listening to a few television/radio news channels. I am content having just enough knowledge to ask reasonably intelligent questions about matters of no real significance to me. I have no need to be a "walking information booth" or to be an icon of wisdom on every subject. Am I advocating an "ignorance is bliss" philosophy? Of course not. I am practicing being secure enough to learn from others. Further, I have found that people will consider you a sparkling conversationalist when all that you have done is asked them questions or allowed them to talk about their favorite subject—themselves.

Notwithstanding, it does wonders for your confidence to be able to converse about a broad range of topics. Again, each person must decide the extent to which he wants to invest the time to secure a large knowledge base. If you are a talk show host, a politician, or work in any other profession where you need to have your finger on the pulse of the world, then delve into the reading material. If not, skim the headlines.

"Knowledge is power" is an even more dynamic truth in the spiritual realm. The satisfaction of acquiring secular knowledge pales in comparison to the emotional security one can achieve from knowing God and His Word. Proverbs 2:6 is a great reminder: "For the LORD gives wisdom; from his mouth come knowledge and understanding."

The more you know about the promises of God, the more confident you'll be. Even if you never become proficient at the secular skills previously discussed, you can still walk in the supreme confidence achieved by connecting with God.

My ongoing prayer is that God will keep aflame my hunger for His Word. Following Solomon's admonishment to "buy the truth" (Proverbs 23:23), I have invested in every possible Bible study aid I can find, from software to books and Bibles to assure full access to and understanding of God's Word.

Daniel reminds us that God "gives wisdom to the wise and knowledge to the discerning. He reveals deep and hidden things; he knows what lies in darkness, and light dwells with him" (Daniel 2:21-22). Yes, the "light," the revelation of the knowledge that we need, does indeed belong to God.

We never have to feel insecure regarding any aspect of our knowledge when we know Him, who knows everything.

In what area of your life (spiritually, vocationally, financially, socially) do you need to enhance your knowledge? What resource will you employ to gain the desired knowledge? When will you start? Whom will you solicit to hold you accountable?

Day 10

The Act of Acceptance

The Elitist Attitude

■ ■ ■ ■

*Belief that you or your group are inherently superior due to
educational, financial, social, religious, or other advantage*

Have you ever alienated someone or deemed her inferior because she
did not share or possess an advantage that you enjoyed? Such elitist thinking is not just a modern-day attitude. As far back as the time of Moses, we
see this mindset displayed.

When God ordered the Jewish elders to appear before Him for a special anointing during the Israelites' journey to the Promised Land, He
poured His Spirit upon all in attendance, and they prophesied. However,
two of the elders stayed in the camp and did not attend. Notwithstanding,
someone saw them prophesying and quickly reported it to Moses.

> Joshua the son of Nun, who had been Moses' aide since youth,
> spoke up and said, "Moses, my lord, stop them!" But Moses
> replied, "Are you jealous for my sake? I wish that all the LORD's
> people were prophets and that the LORD would put his Spirit
> on them!" (Numbers 11:28-29).

Joshua believed only the select group that gathered before the Lord
should prophesy. In the New Testament, we find Jesus rebuking His disciples for their elitist attitude:

> John said to Jesus, "Teacher, we saw someone using your name
> to cast out demons, but we told him to stop because he wasn't
> in our group." "Don't stop him!" Jesus said. "No one who per-
> forms a miracle in my name will soon be able to speak evil of
> me. Anyone who is not against us is for us" (Mark 9:38-40 NLT).

If you are an elitist, you must come to grips with the fact that every advantage or favor you enjoy is a gift from God. Elitism is a form of pride. Humble yourself and realize that what God has given you or allowed you to achieve is for His glory and not your personal exaltation. Even if you think you pulled yourself up by your own bootstraps and achieved your advantage by sheer will and determination, hear the sobering words of the educated and anointed apostle Paul.

> But whatever I am now, it is all because God poured out his
> special favor on me—and not without results. For I have
> worked harder than any of the other apostles; yet it was
> not I but God who was working through me by his grace
> (1 Corinthians 15:10 NLT).

While you may not be an elitist, you must guard against labeling a person or group as elitists simply because they enjoy a certain advantage that you find intimidating and alienating due to your own insecurity or in an attempt to enhance your image to others. This ploy is often used during a political campaign. A candidate may accuse his opponent of elitism simply because he has access to family wealth, graduated from a prestigious university, or has a host of high-profile, influential friends. The opponent so accused attempts to counter the charge by reaching out to blue-collar workers to prove how regular or down-to-earth he is.

In the final analysis, it's not what you *do* but what you *believe* that determines if you have an elitist attitude. I knew a mental health professional who had little regard for the advice of lay counselors. She believed that one had to be a licensed psychologist to give legitimate input.

Maybe it's time to look within. Do you feel superior to others in any aspect of your life? Perhaps you believe that being a part of a particular religious denomination puts you in a special class. Maybe your well-toned body makes you feel superior to the overweight masses. And what if you are well-known in your community? Do you feel you should always be escorted to front-row seats at public gatherings? If so, it's time to bring your attitude into subjection to the Holy Spirit.

The Intolerant Attitude

■ ■ ■ ■

*Refusal to accept people whose views, beliefs, or
lifestyles are different from your own*

We all have a thing or two we can't tolerate. I can't stand for people to chew loudly. I tend to avoid poor communicators who get upset or emotional when somebody does not share their opinion. It irks me when women dress inappropriately for church. It annoys me when preachers and public speakers consistently mispronounce words or use incorrect grammar.

Yes, I admit that I have a pretty extensive list. These kinds of intolerances are fairly common and mostly harmless to others. In my case, they are a reflection of my refusal to extend to others the grace that God extends to me. I've made tremendous progress, but this is an area I consistently target in prayer.

The intolerance that we'll discuss in this chapter is more troublesome to society and to our souls. It is that mean-spirited, hate-filled rejection of people created in God's image simply because they have chosen a certain lifestyle, a particular political affiliation, a religious belief, or other views that we strongly oppose. And yes, racism is also a form of intolerance.

At the outset, let's clarify what tolerance is and what it is not. Tolerance is not about agreeing to embrace differences. It is accepting every person's God-given right, as free moral agents, to believe as he wishes and to behave according to those beliefs so long as his actions do not infringe upon the rights of others or violate established laws.

Whether we choose to love and pray for those whose beliefs and behavior we deem intolerable is a sure test of our emotional and spiritual maturity. When such beliefs violate biblical commands or principles, our response as children of God should be the same as it would be if we were to see a blind man heading for a cliff. Unfortunately today, the typical reaction is to condemn him for going in that direction rather than having compassion and showing him a safer route.

By no means should we view compassion as compromise, any more than we could accuse God, who loves sinners and hates sin, of compromise. Why don't we just emulate our heavenly Father? This does not preclude us from protesting efforts to legalize beliefs and lifestyles that violate Scripture or that we know would be detrimental to society. However, we must be careful not to address these issues with an intolerant attitude.

Let me be more specific. You can be tolerant of the homosexual hairstylist at your salon without compromising your belief that the Bible says homosexual acts are sinful. You can cooperate with your pro-choice coworkers on company projects while being adamantly opposed to abortions. You can respect that your neighbor is a Democrat without ostracizing him as a "bleeding heart liberal" because you are a conservative Republican. You can accept the emotional display during the worship services of certain charismatic churches without judging them to be without substance—merely because you prefer worship services that are more subdued.

Intolerance is not good for society, as evidenced by the resulting crimes, riots, wars, and acts of terrorism, and it's not good for us as individuals. A certain level of agitation and nitpicking accompanies an intolerant attitude. They rob us of our joy and snuff out our light to the world. We would all be wise to heed the words of the late Dr. Edwin Cole who said, "In matters of taste, bend with the wind. In matters of principle, be as firm as a rock."

You can choose to address your intolerant attitude this very moment. Understand that seemingly harmless intolerances, such as the ones I listed at the beginning of this chapter, can create a barrier between you and those God may desire to reach. Ask God to show you when you are attempting to force people to think, act, or believe the way you do. Consider that your own thinking may be flawed in some instances.

Further, when you encounter one of your intolerable targets, be conscious of your negative feelings and consciously resist them. Ask God to replace them with care and concern. In some matters of preference (versus moral standards), you may need to change your beliefs.

Such was the case with Peter. When Cornelius the Gentile summoned him to his home, Peter was extremely reluctant to go. He explained, "You are well aware that it is against our law for a Jew to associate with or visit a Gentile. But God has shown me that I should not call anyone impure or unclean" (Acts 10:28). God was uprooting embedded traditions and opening up new opportunities for the gospel. Peter continued, "I now realize how true it is that God does not show favoritism but accepts from every nation the one who fears him and does what is right" (Acts 10:34-35). Could it be that God wants to expand the borders of your mind for His glory?

The Self-Righteous Attitude

■ ■ ■ ■

*Maintaining a sense of moral superiority; an
exaggerated show of personal holiness*

My friend Debbie was raised in a denomination that taught its members that they were superior to other religious groups because they spoke in tongues and refrained from worldly behaviors such as wearing pants, going to the movies, wearing makeup or nail polish, playing sports (no kidding!), and doing anything else deemed fun. She later learned that some of the leaders who were most adamant about the congregants obeying these strict rules were guilty of adultery, greed, and a host of other sins.

After college, Debbie relocated to another part of the country and joined a church where she was exposed to pants-and-makeup-wearing leaders. It was all very confusing to her as she sat on the sidelines, smugly judging them and the rest of the congregation for their worldly ways. However, she could not deny the power of God at work as they exercised the spiritual gifts of healing, prophecies, miracles, and other manifestations of the Spirit's power.

Finally, Debbie came to realize that many of the convictions she held were a result of man-made traditions; others were issues of personal holiness that God had called her to in order to fulfill His purpose in her life. And yes, some of the members were indeed worldly by any standard, but God had extended His grace to them for reasons that she could not comprehend.

The Pharisees, that religious sect of the Jews who insisted on strict adherence to the law, had a similar mindset to Debbie's. Jesus was quick to denounce it.

Also He spoke this parable to some who trusted in themselves
that they were righteous, and despised others: "Two men went
up to the temple to pray, one a Pharisee and the other a tax
collector. The Pharisee stood and prayed thus with himself,
'God, I thank You that I am not like other men—extortion-
ers, unjust, adulterers, or even as this tax collector. I fast twice
a week; I give tithes of all that I possess.' And the tax collector, standing afar off, would not so much as raise his eyes to
heaven, but beat his breast, saying, 'God, be merciful to me a
sinner!' I tell you, this man went down to his house justified
rather than the other; for everyone who exalts himself will be
humbled, and he who humbles himself will be exalted" (Luke
18:9-14 NKJV).

From this parable, it is clear that God has more tolerance for a repen-
tant sinner than a self-righteous hypocrite. Yes, fasting and tithing were
godly pursuits, but God knew that the Pharisees were guilty of many
sins, including making a show of their righteousness. He spent almost
the entire twenty-third chapter of Matthew denouncing their behavior.

What "good" behavior has been a source of pride for you? Perhaps
you are a hard worker who has gotten fair breaks all of your life and have
never needed any government assistance. Do you negatively judge those
who have? Have you ignored the fact that when you cheated on your
income tax return, you forced the government to give you an involuntary
subsidy? Or maybe you're proud that you have never been unfaithful to
your spouse; you detest those who are sexually immoral. Are you in denial
about the emotional affair at the office, the R-rated movies you watch, or
that quick peek at a pornographic website?

My goal in confronting these issues is not to throw a wet blanket on
our desire for righteousness but to remind us that we all have sinned and
come short of God's requirements. Understand that when we feel good
and righteous, it is because we are close to reaching a man-made standard
versus achieving true intimacy with God. The closer we get to God the
more the light of His Word illuminates the blemishes in our life, and the
more we become aware of our need for His grace and mercy. When we
admit our weaknesses and vulnerabilities, people feel a stronger connection to us and see us as more "relatable."

The very time that I feel like I'm batting a thousand in my spiritual life, an incident will occur that sends me running back to the altar begging forgiveness (usually for unwise words said in haste or a judgmental attitude).

Once when I worked as chief financial officer at a megachurch, one of the most well-dressed women in the congregation bounced a $10 check. I remember going into Pharisee mode: "Lord, I thank You that I am not like Sister Suzy. I have been a faithful tither for over 30 years, and my checks have never bounced because I pursue the right priorities with my money. Besides that I—"

The Lord stopped me mid-sentence. "Do not judge, or you too will be judged" (Matthew 7:1).

It is so easy to get off track. I believe what the Spirit is saying in moments like these is, "Listen, you can't live a godly life in your own strength, so don't be lifted up in pride about the sins you don't commit. Doing right doesn't emanate from your carnal nature. So be merciful and extend to others the grace the Lord extends to you."

So here is a challenge for us all. Let's stop trying to deceive others and ourselves into thinking that our self-righteousness is righteousness. We need to repent of this and all other sins daily. Refuse to judge others by our man-made standards. It is hard to embrace others and to be embraced by them when we are in judgment mode. Pray for those who violate the standards set forth in God's Word. When tempted to judge others, remember that no one can ever be *too bad* for God to use.

The only righteousness we have is from God, and He gave it to us through the blood of Jesus Christ. We can't earn it with our good deeds.

Day 11

Fighting God's Way

Rejecting Carnal Weapons

■ ■ ■ ■

The weapons we fight with are not the weapons
of the world. On the contrary, they have
divine power to demolish strongholds.

2 CORINTHIANS 10:4

Saul found it hard to believe that young David could put an end to the intimidating giant, Goliath. Nevertheless, the timid king suited David for the encounter with his personal armor.

> Then Saul dressed David in his own tunic. He put a coat of armor on him and a bronze helmet on his head. David fastened on his sword over the tunic and tried walking around, because he was not used to them. "I cannot go in these," he said to Saul, "because I am not used to them." So he took them off (1 Samuel 17:38-39).

One of the best strategies when faced with an overwhelming task is to refuse to use carnal weapons. A carnal weapon is any response or solution that springs from your natural inclination. It is in direct opposition to a godly or spiritually inspired alternative. Carnality is the world's way of dealing with the problematic issues of life. Typical examples include lying for gain, seeking revenge, playing dirty politics to get ahead, and other such behaviors. David had not "proven" Saul's heavy armor, but he had "proven" the power of Almighty God. There was no question as to which source of power and protection he was planning to use.

> You come against me with sword and spear and javelin, but I come against you in the name of the LORD Almighty, the God of the armies of Israel, whom you have defied (1 Samuel 17:45).

David knew he could not match the physical strength of Goliath. He also knew he did not have to.

What weapons, methods, or strategies are you "used to" in dealing with your giants? If you are going to tame the emotion of insecurity in your life, you must put off worldly methods of dealing with it. Perfectionism, workaholism, designer clothes, a big house, a fancy car, plastic surgery, or well-connected acquaintances will not cure insecurity. The essence of insecurity is to feel unsure, uncertain, or inadequate. You can only be certain when you connect to the One who has no deficiency.

David had no qualms about admitting his inability to use King Saul's weapons. Most insecure people have a problem with being authentic. They wear a facade of confidence until it becomes a permanent mask.

Secure living requires an honest assessment and acceptance of your personal strengths and weaknesses. If you have made some bad decisions that have gotten you to where you are today, so be it. Don't act like typical victims who refuse to take responsibility for their lives. They would rather blame others for their failures and weaknesses. They may have indeed suffered a genuine inequity or loss at someone's hands. However, like a broken clock, they got stuck in the experience.

Victims have an income statement outlook on life versus a balance sheet view. An income statement is a report of all of the revenues and expenses of an entity for a period of time in the past, such as a month, a quarter, or a year. Everything reported on an income statement represents the past. No subsequent transactions can change that history. What was earned was earned; what was spent was spent. Now the balance sheet, on the other hand, reports the assets and liabilities of an entity as of a specific point in time. As a CPA, I have always been intrigued by the fact that a balance sheet can change the very next day. When you develop a balance sheet mindset, you understand your situation can change without regard to the reality of your past.

You courageously face your liabilities while remaining aware of the fact that you do indeed have some assets. To become emotionally secure, you must have a balanced assessment of what you bring to the table and what your shortcomings are. A proud person, or one who is *pretending* to be secure, focuses only on his assets and buries his head in the sand when it comes to acknowledging his weaknesses. At the other extreme, the insecure person is so focused on his liabilities or shortcomings that he has not developed an appreciation for the attributes or qualities he possesses.

Honestly assessing your strengths and weaknesses is a key step to developing emotional security. Your admitted liability and weakness can be your greatest strength. When you think that you only have assets, the liability that you ignore will ultimately weaken or limit the productivity of your assets.

Below is my personal assessment of my strengths and weaknesses. I invite you to do a personal assessment once you read mine:

Strengths:

- Sincere commitment to God
- Courageous in expressing boundaries
- Good organizer
- Practice integrity in all areas of life
- Strive for excellence in all endeavors
- Comfortable at all social levels
- Formally educated
- Good motivator
- Skilled at conflict management

Weaknesses:

- Impatient with the shortcomings of others
- Often speak too quickly
- Sometimes too direct
- Judge others by their productivity

- Give unsolicited self-improvement advice
- Prone to putting work before relationships

You must embrace what you bring to the table while also acknowledging how your weaknesses impact your daily interactions. This is the truth that will make you free.

David had an intimate relationship with his Father. He knew that the mere name of God is a strong tower where the righteous run to for safety (Proverbs 18:10). No matter what giant he faced, as a "covenant holder" the battle belonged to the Lord. He was secure in that truth.

Forgiving

■ ■ ■ ■

*I focus on this one thing: Forgetting the past
and looking forward to what lies ahead.*

PHILIPPIANS 3:13 NLT

If you are battling unforgiveness, you are probably aware of all the biblical and other reasons why you should forgive someone who has hurt you or someone related to you.

You probably already know that God will not forgive you if you don't forgive an offender. "When you stand praying, if you hold anything against anyone, forgive them, so that your Father in heaven may forgive you your sins" (Mark 11:25). You already know that it would improve your emotional and physical health if you let go of the hurt. You realize your unforgiveness is stressing you because it keeps the memory of the hurtful event fresh in your mind. You may even feel your heart start to race a little each time you rehearse the details, forcing extra adrenaline into your bloodstream. If only the offender could be punished in some manner, not necessarily by you, but in some way that will let him experience the pain you feel. Thoughts of retribution are your constant companions. Stop! Why are you allowing somebody to consume and control your thought life this way? Wouldn't you like the peace of mind that comes from releasing the past and focusing on your future? Let's see how you can break free from Unforgiveness Prison.

One of the most misleading myths about forgiveness is that you can pull it off in your own strength. Someone once said "Forgiveness is divine." There is more to this statement than meets the eye. Forgiveness is not just a good idea; it is a divine mandate that requires divine assistance. Even the *desire* to forgive an offender is God-given. "God is working in you, giving you the desire and the power to do what pleases him" (Philippians 2:13 NLT). Getting to that desire often takes years for some as they like to nurse the grudge, as a mother would a baby. It can only grow with this kind of attention. For God's children, this should not be the case because it is our desire to always do what pleases Him. Therefore, we must ask God for His intervention immediately when someone hurts us. When He gives you the desire to please Him in this regard, it is very likely that you may not feel the emotion of forgiveness. Not to worry. You have made a decision to do the right thing, and the burden is now on your heavenly Father to heal your emotions.

Let's just briefly debunk a couple of other myths about forgiveness. It doesn't mean that you have to resume a relationship with the offender—especially if it is very clear that the person is unrepentant and has not changed his behavior. It also does not mean that you are condoning what he did. You must not think you are letting him off the hook. You are simply disengaging yourself from the hook so that the hurt does not hold you back from the life that is before you. Finally, forget about forgetting. How can you forget? Only God has the capacity to obliterate events from His memory. You will always have the ability to recall the hurtful event if you choose to do so; however, God will take the sting out of it and allow you to not remember it with malice or a desire to see the wrong avenged. You must not let Satan taunt you into thinking you have not forgiven just because you still remember.

Because unforgiveness is such a big problem in the world today between individuals, as well as nations, several secular institutions are studying ways to teach people how to forgive. The Stanford University Forgiveness Project, a long-term study of the impact of forgiveness on mental health, has shown that forgiveness is supreme at reducing chronic stress—the type that eats away at you little by little over time. The researchers have asserted that the ability to forgive is learned behavior. Their methods involve convincing the participants to look for ways to extend understanding to the offender and to find something to be compassionate about. Imagine the impact if they were to introduce the "God factor."

By the way, are *you* one of the past offenders you need to release? Are you so remorseful over a past act that you are stuck and can't forgive yourself? Are you aware that whatever act you perpetrated did not catch God by surprise? Do you know that "everyone has sinned; we all fall short of God's glorious standard" (Romans 3:23)? So why are you keeping yourself in bondage? Release yourself and live!

The Vindictive Attitude

■ ■ ■ ■

Having a strong desire for revenge

A popular phrase says, "Don't get mad, get even!" I'm certain most of us will admit to at least having had a *desire* to avenge a wrong perpetrated against us. Even if we would never do so, we may relish the idea of somebody giving our perpetrator his just dues. I used to hate the very thought that somebody had attempted to hurt or disadvantage me and got away with no apparent consequences.

The Bible is replete with vindictive characters. As I've studied them, I realize none of their lives had a positive ending. Consider Haman, the high-ranking Persian official who sought to exterminate the entire Jewish population because Mordecai the Jew refused to bow to him. His carefully designed plot backfired and resulted in his own death—and that of his ten sons—as well as the granting of his entire estate to Mordecai (Esther 3–9).

And what about the revenge that Absalom, son of King David, took against his half brother Amnon for raping his beloved sister Tamar? Absalom stewed in anger for two years and finally had Amnon murdered at a sheep-shearing party that he hosted for that very purpose. In relating the horrifying event, the king's nephew explained, "Absalom has been plotting this ever since Amnon raped his sister Tamar" (2 Samuel 13:32 NLT). Absalom fled the country. Even though his father permitted him to return after several years, their relationship was never the same. Absalom later attempted to take over the throne and was killed in the long-drawn-out rebellion.

How can you guard against developing a vindictive spirit? Here are some strategies that are sure to quell your temptation to get even.

Stop vocalizing your desire for revenge. "Do not say, 'I will do to them just as they have done to me; I'll pay them back for what they did'" (Proverbs 24:29). Talking about the offense and the offender keeps the emotional wound fresh and the anger brewing. Also, continually discussing the villain with others is a form of retaliation as you get the satisfaction of tarnishing his image.

Put your faith in divine justice. Often a person seeks revenge because he does not believe the justice system or those in authority will adequately address the wrong. Therefore, he takes matters into his own hands. In the story of Absalom's murder of Amnon, King David became angry with Amnon at the time of the rape, but he did nothing to punish him for it. Consequently, Absalom made a decision to redress the wrong himself. This was the beginning of his end.

Refuse to engage in any form of retaliation. Some acts of revenge may not be as severe or significant as the ones above; however, any attempt to avenge a wrong is a violation of God's Word.

Consider what forms of retaliation you've taken to avenge a wrong. Badmouthing the perpetrator? Giving the silent treatment? Making sarcastic remarks? Pretending ignorance to avoid giving assistance on the job? Not showing up? Destroying personal property? Resorting to physical violence or verbal attacks? Taking company resources without authorization? Applying workplace rules more stringently to the offending employee than to others? Deliberately slowing your pace to frustrate the offender? Withholding sex from your spouse?

These are only a few of the behaviors you must resist. God is the only authorized avenger of wrongs. "Do not take revenge, my dear friends, but leave room for God's wrath, for it is written: 'It is mine to avenge; I will repay,' says the Lord" (Romans 12:19).

What I know for sure, after struggling for many years with a vindictive attitude, is that repaying evil for evil will not bring you satisfaction. Besides, have you considered that the person who hurt you may have genuinely changed by now? What if God held your transgressions against you forever? Finally, vindictiveness will destroy your peace of mind because it displeases God. Resist it today!

Day 12

Better Together

Employing Teamwork

■ ■ ■ ■

A person standing alone can be attacked and defeated, but
two can stand back-to-back and conquer. Three are even
better, for a triple-braided cord is not easily broken.

ECCLESIASTES 4:12 NLT

The Lone Ranger, Superwoman, Rambo, and every other "solo phe-nomenon" are no longer viewed as the solution to an insurmountable problem. Teamwork is in. Even some animals practice the power of team-work. For example, though male lions do not usually participate in the hunt for food, the lionesses still get the job done by a system of coopera-tion. They hunt in groups or prides. The majority of the hunting group will chase their prey toward another group lying in wait. This group then engages in a short chase, leaps on the target, and makes the kill. Mission accomplished.

Deuteronomy 32:30 speaks of one chasing a thousand and two put-ting 10,000 to flight. The lesson to be learned is that two working together as a team will be ten times more effective than one going solo. Teams cre-ate synergy. The best explanation of synergy is that a hand is more effective than five fingers working independent of one another. The human body in general is by far the best example of true cooperation. There is not a single bodily activity or function that does not require the cooperation of another part of the body. I thought long and hard about this fact one day and decided to find one activity to refute this theory. I said to myself, "I'll just think, without moving a muscle." Within seconds I realized that I was breathing—a very necessary function for getting oxygen to the brain.

I heard a story about two mountain goats that were coming from opposite sides of the mountain and met each other on a narrow ledge. The ledge was just wide enough for one of them to pass. On one side was the steep wall of the mountain and on the other side was a cliff. The two were facing each other, and there was no room to turn around. It was impossible for either to back up. How do you think they solved their dilemma? If they had been certain people that I know, they would have started butting each other, insisting on their right to pass until they both fell off the cliff. But, as the story goes, these goats exercised more wisdom than that. The first goat decided to lie down and let the second goat literally walk over him. Consequently, they each resumed their trek and reached their destination. Sometimes we have to exercise a little humility to reach our goals.

I know this concept flies in the face of our modern-day mindset of looking out for number one, but I have learned the difference between letting someone walk *over* you versus walking *on* you. You can never be harmed or disadvantaged by someone stepping *over* you. No one can block your destiny. Now, only people with low self-evaluation will allow people to step *on* them. Walking over me will not diminish or disadvantage me. The first goat's decision to humble himself assured that he would reach *his* goal.

At a team-building seminar I attended some time ago, the leader kept admonishing us to remember that "none of us is as smart as all of us." I'm not sure if he authored the phrase, but I will never forget the reality of it. I repeat it often.

If you are trying to build a team, you must be careful that as a leader you do not sabotage the group's effectiveness by catering to or rewarding prima donnas. Whether something good or bad happens, the entire team should share the glory or the pain. In the heartwarming movie *Coach Carter*, the no-nonsense high school basketball coach imposed an impossible physical training penalty on one of the talented but rebellious players who had quit the team because he did not want to submit to the coach's strict disciplines. After a time, the player began to miss interacting with the group and the opportunity to be a part of a now-winning team. He wanted in again. The coach agreed to allow him to rejoin the team on one condition: He had to complete an extraordinary number of push-ups and "suicide runs" by a certain date. All of the exercises had to be done during regular team practice under the watchful eye of the coach's assistant. On the final day, the penitent student was not able to reach his goal. The coach told him to hit the road.

At that moment, a funny thing happened. One by one, each member of the team, now understanding what it meant to work together, slowly volunteered to complete his requirement. The coach, heartened by their show of unity, allowed it and the player rejoined the team. The group went on to achieve unprecedented success.

Of course, not every leader is like Coach Carter. I have seen insecure bosses deliberately create dissension among members of their staff. Obviously, they feared that if the employees worked in harmony, they would unite against them. Management is certainly not for cowards or insecure people. What about you? On a scale of one to ten, ten being highest, how effective a team player are you? Consider a significant improvement you can implement starting today.

Engaging Constructive Feedback

■ ■ ■ ■

*Whoever loves discipline loves knowledge, but
he who hates correction is stupid.*

PROVERBS 12:1

No one has 20-20 vision on himself; thus, no one exercises total objectivity in evaluating his own behavior. Notwithstanding, we all need feedback for personal growth and development. We will often find ourselves challenged with being either the recipient or the giver of such helpful communication. Unfortunately, insecure people do not seek or readily give constructive feedback. They are afraid of negative responses.

I had an interesting experience in the workplace once when I headed an editing committee whose responsibility was to make sure that the company's annual report of operations was a quality production. The report was a compilation of narratives written by various department managers.

Assuming that all those who had contributed to the report were working toward the same goal, the committee freely edited out bad grammar, misspellings, extraneous information, and other violations of the rules of effective writing. Big mistake! Many of the contributors were offended by the modifications. Tempers flared. I was flabbergasted to see people who viewed corrections as personal attacks. I felt my career plane had just experienced a crash landing in "Insecurityville." God sustained me through that experience. I continue to thank Him that I have been drilled during my professional career to always solicit a second pair of eyes on any worthwhile project.

Giving constructive feedback can be perceived as either a negative or a positive undertaking. The objective should always be to enhance or develop some aspect of a person's life or performance. Unfortunately, if the receiver has low self-worth, any pointing out of a weakness may be met with defensiveness, resentment, rejection, or even hostility. Consequently, most people are reluctant to saying anything at all. However, if we really care about somebody, we must take the chance, for their sake, to help them develop.

The ability to provide effective feedback is learned behavior. The more we practice it, the better we become at it. Let's look at four practical, God-honoring ways to provide helpful input.

Prayerfully. Pray before you decide to approach someone with constructive feedback. Ask God to reveal your true motive. Are you angry with the person and wanting to get something off your chest? Are you just being critical in order to make yourself feel better about your own shortcomings and insecurities? Once you are clear as to your motives, you must pray that the person will be receptive to your input. Think about what you will say. Get God's guidance. Pray that the words He will give you will have the right impact. "So is my word that goes out from my mouth: It will not return to me empty, but will accomplish what I desire and achieve the purpose for which I sent it" (Isaiah 55:11).

Promptly. Don't delay to give needed feedback. The situation will only continue, and maybe even get worse, when the person is not aware of his shortcoming. Prompt feedback will enable you to more accurately cite specific instances of the problematic behavior. Of course, it would be helpful to be prepared to offer specific suggestions for improvement.

Personally. Go directly to the person yourself—always face-to-face when possible. No one appreciates knowing you have shared his short-comings with everybody else in his circle of interaction before you told him. Own the problem. Tell him what you have observed personally. Don't hide behind what "they" are saying. Ideally, you will have already demonstrated your support toward the person long before you decide you need to "fix" him. This will certainly help him to be more receptive to your input.

Privately. Be sure that no one else is around to hear the feedback. Giving feedback in the presence of others will only cause the person to be concerned with saving face; there is a good chance he will not absorb a word you say. Don't be disappointed if the person doesn't immediately embrace your feedback. Sometimes the truth is too painful to be accepted quickly. Express your care and support and leave the rest to God. You've done your job.

No one enjoys hearing about his weaknesses. If you are ever going to walk in confidence, then you must learn how to benefit from such input. Allow me to give you four tips for responding to not-so-pleasant information.

Listen. Do not interrupt with an explanation or excuse for your behavior. Know that your defensiveness is often resistance to the pain of the truth. "If you listen to constructive criticism, you will be at home among the wise" (Proverbs 15:31 NLT).

Look. Check to see if there is a kernel of truth. "To one who listens, valid criticism is like a gold earring" (Proverbs 25:12 NLT). There is usually some modicum of truth to negative input—especially when you hear it from more than one person. Don't be afraid of the truth; it will set you free.

Learn. Be open to new ways to behave. Ask for suggestions. Teachableness is a godly trait. "Instruct the wise and they will be wiser still; teach the righteous and they will add to their learning" (Proverbs 9:9).

Leave. You don't have to entertain groundless criticism. Simply say, "Thank you for your input." Learn to handle feedback much the way you eat bony fish; eat the flesh and leave the bones. Let all of the "confidence zapping" comments and accusations hurled your way hit your shield of faith rather than absorbing them into your emotions. We must keep our spiritual armor intact and not let criticism penetrate our soul, mind, will, or emotions.

Now is a good time to write a brief script of what you will say to someone whom you have been planning or desiring to give constructive feedback. How you would feel or respond if you were the recipient of this input?

Solidifying Your Support System

■ ■ ■ ■

A friend loves at all times, and a brother
is born for a time of adversity.

PROVERBS 17:17

No man is an island. No man stands alone. Just as God created our physical bodies in such a way that our various internal systems support one another, so it is in our relationships. Everybody needs a support system. Many times, when a person's pride is working overtime, or when he has experienced what he feels is an unforgivable hurt at the hands of friends, family members, or his church family, he will decide to write off the whole human race and try to go it alone. "It's just going to be God and me from now on," he may declare. Big mistake! No one should attempt to deal with the pressures of life in isolation. I believe that isolation is one of Satan's most effective strategies. He has a clear shot when there is no one to help you block his fiery darts. "A person standing alone can be attacked and defeated, but two can stand back-to-back and conquer. Three are even better, for a triple-braided cord is not easily broken" (Ecclesiastes 4:12 NLT).

I knew a young lady who had a baby out of wedlock. She also had a very demanding job. Unfortunately, she had no support system. She did not have a warm and friendly personality, rarely extended herself to others, and had not invested in the kind of relationships where people were aware of and willing to help her when problems arose. She often found herself in a dilemma when her child needed to be picked up from day care or required other special attention at times that she was not able to get off from work. King Solomon admonished, "A man who has friends must himself be friendly" (Proverbs 18:24 NKJV).

I know firsthand the value and benefit of support when one is under stress. Not only do I have a supportive husband, but I also come from a large family who will come to my rescue at the drop of a hat. Beyond just having someone to commiserate with about the problem, it is great to know they care about the outcome. Study after study has shown that people who have caring support live longer, recover from illnesses faster, and find life more meaningful. Support gives us a sense of connection and acceptance that are core human needs. Support provides an arena in which you can be vulnerable, a place where you can feel safe in saying, "I don't know," "Can you help me?" and "I need a hug." This is support God's way.

In an ideal world, our primary support would come from our family. However, if this is not your reality, don't despair and don't get stuck wishing it were so. God has made provision for you through church fellowship groups, people with common interests, coworkers, and other groups. You must take the initiative in reaching out and establishing meaningful relationships.

As you seek to solidify your support system, keep in mind that support must be mutual. "Share each other's troubles and problems, and in this way obey the law of Christ" (Galatians 6:2). Nothing is more detrimental to a support system than for it to become one-sided. Don't become so engulfed in your own issues that you forget your supporters are also dealing with the pressures of life. Inquire about and genuinely listen to their concerns. Nobody likes a taker. I had a friend who absolutely could not listen to my issues for more than a few minutes before she would interrupt and turn the conversation into an endless discussion of her problems. I pointed out to her several times her tendency to do this, but she never changed. It was so frustrating. I finally became "too busy" to continue the relationship.

Finally, do not forget to express tangible appreciation for those who support you. Cards and token gifts on special occasions go a long way in saying, "I acknowledge and appreciate your help." Don't allow your support system to fall apart because of lack of nourishment on your part. God doesn't want you to walk on the dangerous ground of isolation.

Day 13

Clarifying Expectations

Establishing Boundaries

■ ■ ■ ■

"If you do not obey these commands," declares the LORD,
"I swear by myself that this palace will become a ruin."

JEREMIAH 22:5

We all have limits, relational lines that we don't want people to cross. Some people are very direct in expressing such boundaries, while others are too fearful of rejection and alienation to communicate them. Setting boundaries can be a risky undertaking, and sometimes it requires real emotional security to take the plunge.

Boundaries help us to define the parameters of our personal and professional lives. They will keep us emotionally and physically healthy. Many insecure people make sacrifices for others to the point of resentment. No one should ever make a habit of sacrificing grudgingly or unwillingly—not even for the Lord Himself. The psalmist admonishes us to "worship the LORD with gladness" (Psalm 100:2).

If you want to accelerate your growth in the area of setting boundaries, you must immediately begin saying no to activities that bring you no enjoyment and that do not fit into your divine purpose for your life. In Luke 12:14 we read the story of a man who asked Jesus to mediate a property dispute between him and his brother regarding their inheritance. Jesus simply replied, "Man, who appointed me a judge or an arbiter between you?" In other words, Jesus was saying, "I'm staying in My lane.

I am not going to allow you to distract Me from My purpose by getting involved in something I have not been called to do." The additional lessons to be learned from the incident are (1) Jesus didn't give a long explanation as to why He couldn't oblige them, and (2) He did not say He wasn't available *right now.* Such a response always leaves the door open for a subsequent request.

If you are just starting to develop your sense of security, you may be more comfortable responding to an undesirable request by stating, "I'm sorry. I have a prior commitment." You may be wondering, "Suppose I do not have a commitment?" Indeed you do. You have made a commitment to yourself to stop being manipulated into doing things you do not want to do!

When we fail to express our boundaries, people become unclear as to what behavior will be accepted or tolerated by us. They are left to decide for themselves based upon their own preferences, convenience, or whims.

God has made us stewards over the following three areas of our lives where the lines of interaction can become blurry if we do not clearly define them:

Our time. Time discriminates against no one. We all get 1440 minutes each day. If we do not structure our days according to our desired priorities, we will constantly find ourselves frustrated and wondering where our time went. Many people will tolerate chaos or disorganization to avoid being unpopular with those who do not embrace structure or change. In one of my management positions, I had to abandon my "open door" policy when the long lines and distractions started to render me ineffective and nearly drove me crazy.

On the home front, because my husband is an early riser, I set boundaries by informing all of my friends and family to refrain from calling our home after 10 p.m. except for emergencies. When they violate the boundary, they get the answering machine.

Our talent. It is personally rewarding and esteem-boosting to know you have a skill or talent other people need and desire. However, it can also be a source of frustration when others conclude that they have a right to freely use your talent simply for the asking. As a CPA I receive numerous calls requesting financial services which I could indeed render if I wanted to work 24 hours a day. Some are from friends of friends or family members who are hoping I will do the work pro bono. Occasionally, I will volunteer an hour or so of brain-picking. However, I have found that people place little value on anything gotten free. Therefore, I often refer them to professionals who can accommodate their needs.

Our treasure. The financial arena is one of the most challenging areas of setting boundaries. Long-term relationships can be dissolved over a transaction gone bad. Heed the following advice on setting financial boundaries.

- Discuss with your spouse the maximum dollar amount that each of you may spend without getting the other's permission. Agree that any amount above this limit will be considered "major" and will require complete agreement.

- Establish a general policy of no loans to family members. If you decide to make an exception to the policy, make sure your spouse is in complete agreement. Put terms and due dates in writing.

- Don't enable your child, spouse, or anyone else to remain irresponsible by bailing him out or always being his safety net. This is the best strategy for implementing one of God's most effective teaching tools—sowing and reaping the consequences of individual behavior.

It is time to break the habit of doing more and more things you do not really want to do—and resenting every moment of it. The key is to start small with an issue you perceive has very little risk of loss or impact on the respective relationship. It may be as simple as deciding to pay only your share of a restaurant bill rather than splitting the entire thing with fellow friends or family who ordered as if there were no tomorrow.

As we become secure enough to establish our personal boundaries, we must also go a step further and express the consequences we are willing to put into action when someone violates them. After all, boundaries without consequences are just wishes. Wishes will not change anybody's behavior toward us.

Is there an area of your life where you need to set a boundary? Why haven't you done so? What do you really fear?

Evaluating Your Expectations

■ ■ ■ ■

Yes, my soul, find rest in God; my hope comes from him.

PSALM 62:5 KJV

We all have expectations of those in our circle of interaction—whether on the job, in the home, at church, or in our social lives. Many times we may not be totally aware of them, do not express them, or will not acknowledge that they are unrealistic. Therefore, they can cause us a great deal of frustration and therefore stress.

Consider the story of Mary and her friend Joan who were having brunch with a group of friends one Sunday after church. Everyone was talking about the success of a project that Mary had just completed. Out of the clear blue, Joan started a completely different conversation with the woman sitting next to her just as Mary was making a remark. Mary was annoyed by her rudeness but playfully chided, "Hey, wait a minute. We already have a conversation going here!" Joan retorted, "I don't believe in one person being the center of a conversation." Her comment really offended Mary, but to maintain her reputation for being gracious, Mary simply smiled and dropped the matter while Joan resumed her sidebar conversation. Mary could feel the increase in her heart rate as she sat there frustrated by the disrespect and inconsideration of someone who claimed to be her friend. She mentally decided to refrain from inviting Joan to any future social functions and vowed to be "too busy" for any invitations Joan extended to her.

Failed expectations will always create stress if we allow them. Mary's expectation of Joan was not an unrealistic one—unlike Donna, who becomes extremely frustrated each week when her housekeeper fails to arrange her pictures on the fireplace mantle in the exact same angle after dusting them. "All she has to do is to pay attention," she complains. "Is that too much to ask?" This really stresses Donna—especially since the house-keeper just presented her with an unjustifiable increase for her services.

In a final scenario, consider John, who worked from home. When his wife would arrive home from the office each evening, he would still be working at his computer. "Honey, I'm home!" she would yell. He would yell back "Hello" without even looking up until she came into the office where he was. It really annoyed her that he would not get up and greet her at the door. He would sometimes sense her change in mood and ask, "Is something wrong?" "Nope," she would respond, while silently thinking, *He should know to get up and greet me. Do I have to teach him everything?*

The scenarios are endless. Unfortunately, some of the most harmful and stress-producing expectations are the ones we have of ourselves. "I should be able to raise three children, have dinner on the table each night, work ten-hour days, and be perfectly coiffed when my husband walks in the door." And why, may I ask, *should* you? Expectations will keep you locked into a stress-filled life in "Shoulds Prison" where everything goes and everybody behaves as he *should*.

Let's do a little exercise to put our expectations in perspective. You can start with your immediate family (spouse, children, siblings, parents) and list your key expectations of each person. Try to be objective in assessing whether they are realistic. Understand the origin or core reason for an expectation. Have you shared these expectations? If not, why not? Do you fear the parties' reactions? What is the worst that could happen? Are you willing to negotiate some of your expectations? I say *negotiate* rather than *eliminate* because in some instances you may need to continue to maintain high expectations of others or they may not have the motivation to move to another level of excellence. Notwithstanding, to preserve your peace, there may be instances in which you may have to eliminate certain expectations—especially when they involve matters of preference versus issues which are immoral or illegal.

I know a woman whose father has never said to her "I love you," even though she says it to him at the end of each of their conversations. He simply replies, "Okay." She needs to understand that he cannot (or will not) meet her expectation because, though he does indeed love her, he is uncomfortable or emotionally incapable of saying "I love you." This is an expectation she needs to abandon.

Complete the expectation exercise for each of your key environments. What are your expectations of your boss? Do you expect him to manage your career? Do you expect your company to always be loyal to you and to never consider downsizing you out of the organization? Is this realistic? Nope. Not in today's corporations. It's not personal; it's just business. Moving along to your church, what expectations do you have of your pastor? For example, do you expect him to visit every hospitalized member of the church? This may be realistic for a 200 member congregation, but if the church's membership has now reached mega status, a visit from an assigned individual may be the norm.

Please know that in order to maintain your peace of mind, you are going to have to expect less of people and more of God. Do not set yourself up to be frustrated. Bring all of your expectations before Him for evaluation. Let Him weed out the unrealistic ones. Let Him give you the courage to express the ones that need to be communicated. Trust Him to influence the hearts of those involved so that your expectations do not become a source of stress for you or for them.

Asking for What You Want

■ ■ ■ ■

You do not have because you do not ask God.

JAMES 4:2

Some people know what they want and have the courage to ask for it. Others know what they do not want and have developed the skill of expressing it in a manner that does not create hostility. Both groups have learned that expressing your wishes is one of the key strategies for managing stress.

When Daniel, the Hebrew captive, was required to eat the nonkosher foods provided by his Babylonian captors, he did not stress out about what to do. "But Daniel resolved not to defile himself with the royal food and wine, and he asked the chief official for permission not to defile himself this way" (Daniel 1:8). His request was granted, and he and his three friends were permitted to eat a vegetarian diet—with great physical and intellectual success.

I recently went down to the Los Angeles wholesale shopping district to make a few quick purchases. When I arrived, I discovered to my dismay that I had not brought my wallet, which contained my driver's license, checkbook, and credit cards. I only had a change purse and my cell phone, which incorporates various contact information. On the contact list I had included coded information for my most frequently used credit card. I knew that the chances were pretty slim that a vendor would allow me to make a purchase based solely upon the card number and expiration date—with no identification and no actual card. Los Angeles was in the midst of a record-breaking heat wave, and I greatly needed a cool but professional outfit for a very important meeting that would start in a few hours. Notwithstanding, I did not want the stress of making the trip back home to get my wallet and then returning downtown in all of the traffic. I appealed to a certain vendor to trust me. She relented, took down the credit card information, and allowed me to buy the outfit. I proceeded to the next vendor and showed him the receipt as evidence that I had already been trusted by one of his fellow vendors. He allowed me to make a purchase as well. I completed four purchases that day, including one for "cash only." God gave me favor, and I convinced reluctant vendor number three (where I shopped often) to charge my credit card for a certain amount of cash over and above the amount of my purchase in order for me to complete transaction number four. It pays to ask.

Even in more serious matters of life, if you do not practice asking for what you want, you will live a life of frustration and resentment if you decide that people should discern your needs, preferences, or desires without telling them. Some people daily allow others to violate their boundaries while they suffer in silence rather than asking for a change in the stressor's behavior.

Asking for what you want is probably most difficult in a work environment. Never assume that your well-being is uppermost in your boss's mind. This is not an indictment against her. She's too occupied with her own issues. If you are a salaried employee and have been consistently working many hours of uncompensated overtime, try asking for a special bonus for a portion of the amount that it would have cost the company had they paid you for the time. Present a well-thought-out analysis, or ask for some time off equal to a portion of what the hours would convert to in terms of days. Better still, request more staff to help you do the work. Pray and decree the favor of God before you ask. If your request is denied, consider what that is telling you about the company. Of course, if the company is experiencing a financial crisis, you should understand and stick with time-off requests. Whatever you do, do not adopt a negative attitude. Keep being excellent at your work and start thinking of Plan B for your career. Sometimes management's decisions serve to motivate us to go to the next step in God's sovereign plan for our lives.

Practice expressing your boundaries or preferences in a calm, non-hostile manner. Resist the cowardly temptation to engage in hints or indirect forms of communication—at home or at work. If you are a manager and have supervisors under your charge, be clear on what you want and don't want. Phrases such as "I'd like…" "Would you kindly…" and "I'd appreciate it if you'd…" will go a long way in communicating your desires without making you sound hostile and demanding. Most of all, such an approach will relieve you of the stress of wondering, "When will he ever get a clue?"

One of the most unique attributes that God has given to us as humans is the ability to communicate. We do not have to stress out wishing or hoping that someone will read our minds when we could just ask for what we want.

Day 14

Taming Tension

Rejecting Pride

■ ■ ■ ■

God opposes the proud, but shows favor to the humble.

1 Peter 5:5 nkjv

Pride can destroy your life faster than a speeding bullet. This inordinate sense of superiority has been at the root of some of the world's greatest tragedies. The Scriptures are filled with stories of pride and its deadly consequences. It was because of pride that Lucifer tried to exalt himself above God and in so doing persuaded a host of angels to rebel in heaven (Isaiah 14). It was pride that caused Ahithophel to commit suicide because Absalom did not take his advice (2 Samuel 17:23). Pride caused Haman to plot the death of Mordecai and all the Jews because Mordecai would not bow to him (Esther 3:5). God brought disaster on the prosperous coastal city of Tyre to destroy their pride and to "bring into contempt all the honorable of the earth" (Isaiah 23:8 kjv).

Benjamin Franklin said, "There is perhaps not one of our natural passions so hard to subdue as pride. Beat it down, stifle it, mortify it as much as one pleases, it is still alive. Even if I could conceive that I had completely overcome it, I should probably be proud of my humility."

Because God opposes the proud, a person who walks in pride cannot experience a close, intimate, and confidence-producing relationship with Him. Their pride blinds them to their insignificance when compared to

Almighty God. Their estimation of themselves is as out of proportion as the flea who told the elephant, "Brace yourself. I'm about to jump off!"

God will not tolerate pride from anyone. If the self-exalted one refuses to humble himself, he leaves God with no other choice than to do it for him. The story of how King Nebuchadnezzar's pride caused him to fall from the palace to the pit of insanity is a prime example (see Daniel 4).

Pride promotes self-reliance. It tells us we can indeed do things on our own. In our attempt to walk in self-confidence, we slam the door in God's face and shut out the work of the Holy Spirit, our helper. The apostle Paul could boast of being educated, sophisticated, and consecrated, yet he humbly declared, "By the grace of God I am what I am, and his grace to me was not without effect. No, I worked harder than all of them—yet not I, but the grace of God that was with me" (1 Corinthians 15:10).

For many years I was in hot pursuit of self-confidence. I embraced the teachings of secular motivational speakers who convinced me that if I believed in *myself,* the sky was the limit in terms of what I could accomplish. However, having faced several professional and personal situations that required greater skills, knowledge, and mental fortitude than I possessed, I began to realize that my self-confidence was woefully inadequate. Smarts can only take you so far. I needed to rely on something or someone bigger and better equipped. I quickly learned that self-confidence is an unstable foundation. Jesus warned, "Apart from me you can do nothing" (John 15:5). Since we can indeed do nothing apart from Him, it seems that the focus of our energies should be on getting as close to Him as possible.

Sometimes we become so confident because of our track record that we assume we will always be victorious in a certain area. Pastor Frank Wilson tells the story of a church that was so impressed with a certain deacon's years of humble service that they voted to award him a "badge of humility." They were chagrined the next Sunday when he came to church sporting it on the lapel of his suit. The pastor graciously took it away from him.

We are most likely to fall, most apt to be blindsided, and most apt to be caught off guard when we are most confident of our own strength. Paul warns, "If you think you are standing firm, be careful that you don't fall!" (1 Corinthians 10:12).

It just doesn't pay to brag or even to be subtly proud of our strengths. For instance, I always asserted that I could keep my cool in any emotionally charged situation. I have practiced for years staying calm and responding in an even tone. During a conversation with a friend, I reiterated that this was indeed a strong suit that had worked for me. Within a few days of our discussion, a colleague pushed a button I didn't even know I had. I found myself yelling at him at the top of my voice. I had never done that before or since. I will never be able to boast of this strength again. Since then, I have ceased claiming any personal strong suits. I've decided to follow Paul's example. "That is why, for Christ's sake, I delight in weaknesses…in difficulties. For when I am weak, then I am strong" (2 Corinthians 12:10).

By no means am I suggesting that we should go around talking about how weak we are. I am simply cautioning that we must stay *mindful* that our strength in any situation is dependent upon God and not on our own ability.

Are you challenged by a proud spirit? What, exactly, is the object of your pride (a particular accomplishment, physical attractiveness, a talent)? It is time to let the Holy Spirit empower you to reject this insidious emotional enemy.

Resolving Conflicts

■ ■ ■ ■

*If your brother or sister sins, go and point out
their fault, just between the two of you. If they
listen to you, you have won them over.*

MATTHEW 18:15

There are few things I find more stress-generating than unresolved conflict. It keeps my adrenaline on high alert and consumes my thoughts until I have resolved it. Consequently, I try to confront offenses and misunderstandings right away. Not all people feel this way. Even though Jesus commanded us to initiate a reconciliation with an offending brother, many Christians believe that we are to keep quiet for "peace's sake." If we are going to manage the stress in our lives, we must develop the skills needed to address the conflicts which are sure to arise—for conflicts are indeed inevitable. Further, the problem with failing to confront an issue is that it is likely to occur again.

I have set forth below some basic guidelines for resolving conflict that, if practiced, should result in a harmonious outcome:

- Ask God to give you His words to say so that His purpose will be achieved. "My word…will not return to me empty, but will accomplish what I desire and achieve the purpose for which I sent it" (Isaiah 55:11).

- Empty your anger or other emotions out to God before engaging the offender. Emotions tend to get in the way of the facts and can hinder objective thinking. This isn't as hard as it may sound once you decide you are going to make every effort to settle the issue in a harmonious way. "If it is possible, as far as it depends on you, live at peace with everyone" (Romans 12:18).

- Be clear as to what you perceive the problem to be. Avoid vague statements that leave room for misinterpretation. For example, "You need to do better" does not really clarify the problem.

- Focus the discussion on the offender's behavior and avoid remarks about his character. For example: "It was inappropriate for you to open my private mail" is better than saying, "I can't believe you are so nosey!"

- Stay open-minded and always seek first to understand the other person's behavior rather than justifying your own. Obviously, this will require effective listening on your part. Listening will validate the other person's feelings and give him incentive to listen to you.

- Resolve one issue at a time. Do not cloud the discussion with other unresolved matters between you. Deal with them later.

- Agree on future behavior should the situation arise again.

Strife is stressful, and it is to our advantage to keep it at bay. We cannot eliminate conflicts from our lives because we are all unique individuals with different backgrounds, communication styles, and preferences. However, we can confront the issues, resolve them, and grow as a result.

Releasing Your Tension

■ ■ ■ ■

Be still, and know that I am God.

Psalm 46:10

In addition to walking, running, or other physical activities, we must practice ways to release the tension that builds up in us when we experience temporary stress. I have set forth a few strategies below that I find to be pretty effective.

Take a deep breath. I don't know about you, but sometimes when I'm working at warp speed or something is going on that threatens to stress me, I find that my breathing becomes shallow. Other times it seems I literally forget to breathe. Taking a deep breath can do wonders in diffusing the tension you may be feeling. Deep breathing relaxes you because it lowers your heart rate and circulates extra oxygen to various parts of the body. Here's the scoop on how to get the most out of it. I'm not sure where I first learned this, but I have practiced it for years.

Breathe deeply. Inhale rather loudly and slowly through your nostrils (mouth closed) counting to ten. Fill your diaphragm area as if it were a balloon. Listen only to your breathing; it should sound like the ocean. Exhale slowly through your mouth, making a hissing sound with your teeth together. Listen only to your breathing. Take ten seconds to exhale. Repeat five to ten times throughout the day, depending on the amount of stress you are feeling. Obviously, this exercise has to be done in private; however, if you feel you need to do it immediately, just skip the sound effects and breathe quietly but deeply. This is also a good exercise to do when you get into bed at night. When done with the sound effects, it can be very effective in shutting down your overactive mind.

Squeeze a stress ball or gadget. These come in several shapes. I have one shaped like a cell phone, another like a mini-calculator, and one like a tennis ball. Simply squeezing it as tightly as you'd like relieves tension. These are usually available at an office supply store.

Blow a whistle. I attended a celebration recently, and as part of the festivities all the guests received a paper funnel horn to blow at certain intervals during the program. I left the horn in my car and forgot about it.

Shortly thereafter, I was driving down the street and became so exasperated with insensitive, bad drivers that I just pulled the paper horn from the side pocket of the door and blew it with all my might. What a relief! Of course, the windows were up and no one heard it except me. Any whistle will do the trick!

Sing. When Paul and Silas were jailed for preaching the gospel, they chose to sing. "Around midnight, Paul and Silas were praying and singing hymns to God, and the other prisoners were listening to them" (Acts 16:25). I have found that a nice worship song ushers me into the presence of God and floods my soul with peace.

Self-massage. Learn to massage your tense areas yourself. If you find it a little difficult to reach your shoulders and neck effectively, put a small baseball in a long sock and lean against it on a wall while holding the top of the sock with your hand. You can control the intensity of the pressure by how hard you press against the wall. This also feels great on the lower back.

These are just a few of the positive strategies you can employ in lieu of drumming your fingers, complaining, and engaging in other unproductive habits.

Day 15

Sharing the Power

Empowering Others

■ ■ ■ ■

When Jesus had called the Twelve together, he gave
them power and authority to drive out all demons
and to cure diseases, and he sent them out to proclaim
the kingdom of God and to heal the sick.

LUKE 9:1-2

Emotionally secure people seek to empower others. Jesus masterfully empowered His disciples. "Very truly I tell you, whoever believes in me will do the works I have been doing, and they will do even greater things than these, because I am going to the Father" (John 14:12). He ensured that His mission on earth would continue to be accomplished long after He was gone. When we make it a habit to empower others, we energize them to reach their goals and ours.

Successful retailers know that when they empower frontline clerks to resolve customers' issues, they create a win-win situation. Repeat customers enjoy the no-hassle policy and the sales assistants feel more fulfilled in their jobs.

Some managers, on the other hand, use lack of empowerment as a means for controlling their employees. Unfortunately, these managers sabotage the company's effectiveness and profitability. The principles of empowerment work the same in our personal lives and our work world. Let's look at few strategies for empowering others.

Inform/Train. There is nothing more demoralizing, disempowering, and esteem-robbing than being kept out of the loop on information that impacts you. As difficult as it must have been to get His disciples to understand, Jesus knew He had to inform them of events to come that would affect them. "The Son of Man is going to be delivered into the hands of men," He said. "They will kill him, and after three days he will rise" (Mark 9:31).

If we accept the truism "Information is power," you would think that everybody would use this tool to empower others. Unfortunately, some people withhold information as a means of controlling others. They use uncertainty to keep the employee guessing about his plight. Keeping employees in the dark on key issues sabotages productivity and creativity. Further, employees who receive company-sponsored training tend to be more loyal and productive. Such an investment in them gives them a sense of being valued and thereby meets a basic human need. When they feel good about themselves, they will feel good about the company and seek ways to return the favor.

The need to be informed is not limited to the workplace. Many stay-at-home wives do not feel empowered, as some of them have no knowledge of and no say in the family finances. Both spouses need to understand that they are in a partnership and that each needs to be involved with major financial decisions and have a general understanding of monthly income and expenditures.

Trust. Empowerment occurs when you trust people with a task without micromanaging them. Empowerment is simply loosing the reins over *how* something is going to be done while retaining control over *what* should be done. Corporate management gurus all agree that employees perform better when given freedom to perform their jobs with some level of independence.

In a marriage, a wise woman empowers her husband when she demonstrates that she trusts his decision making. One of my mentors, considering my strong personality, gave me some sage advice early in my marriage on how to empower my husband. She warned, "Whatever you do, he won't do." What she meant was that if I want my husband to be strong in an area, I must resist the temptation to take it over and handle it for him. This was some of the best input I have ever received.

Care. Showing that you care about people beyond what they can do for you is an act of empowerment. In these modern times of downsizing, rightsizing, and precipitous cutbacks to achieve bottom-line results, employee loyalty is at an all-time low. While you may have no direct control over certain company decisions, if you are a manager or supervisor, the least you can do is to show your staff that you care by occasional lunches out and taking an interest in their private lives.

Appreciate. I often muse over the fact God made us in His image. Therefore, I believe we share many of His desires. For instance, He wants us to praise, thank, and appreciate Him for His goodness. We too want to be praised, thanked, and appreciated for the good we have done. Hardly anything is more demoralizing than feeling unappreciated. Sincere praise energizes a person and causes him to spring up like a wilted flower that's just been watered. Practice appreciating good workers and expressing your belief in their skills and abilities. Understand that a paycheck is not the only motivator.

Several years ago, I began leaving friends and family members voice-mails just expressing how grateful I am to have them in my life and giving specific praise for things they have done or for things I admire about them. One friend told me she kept the message on her answering machine so that she could replay it for occasional encouragement—and an oasis from her verbally abusive husband.

Oh, the dividends that a husband or wife or anyone else would reap from expressing appreciation for the little things. Just in case your gratitude muscle has grown weak and you take most kindnesses and efforts for granted, make a list of some possible tasks or responsibilities to appreciate your spouse for performing (example, taking out the trash, getting the car washed, supporting your career, etc.).

Why not set a goal of appreciating at least one thing per day for a particular person in your life? If you are a man, don't be so insecure that you fear you will appear weak if you start to notice the little things. It takes a real man to look beyond his needs and recognize the efforts of another.

When you walk in emotional security, you look for ways to give people more power by keeping them informed, trusting them, caring about them, or appreciating them. It will bring greater balance to your life as well as raise the esteem and productivity of the empowered one.

Has fear kept you from empowering someone in your circle of interaction? What will you do today to start reversing this behavior?

Preserving Preeminence

■ ■ ■ ■

Diotrephes, who loves to be first, will not welcome us.

3 JOHN 9

Have you ever had the distinction of being the "only," the "first," or "one of the few" individuals to accomplish a particular goal or to achieve a certain level of success in a certain environment? Perhaps you hold an honored or highly esteemed position at your church, workplace, or other social setting. You may even have a reputation for being the most skilled, knowledgeable, or highly regarded person in a particular discipline. Whatever the situation, life atop the pedestal can be a heady experience—until someone comes along and threatens to topple you. Whether leader or layman, an insecure individual will resort to almost any means necessary to protect his position or to preserve his place of preeminence.

The apostle John was eager to spread the gospel and to strengthen the new Christians. He wrote and asked Diotrephes, a New Testament church leader, to allow certain ministers to come and preach at his church. Diotrephes flatly denied John's request. John was extremely disappointed with Diotrephes's response and related the incident to his friend Gaius in a subsequent letter. "I wrote to the church, but Diotrephes, who loves to be first, will not welcome us" (3 John 9). Diotrephes viewed the traveling ministers as competitors who would threaten his position in his church. Therefore, he not only refused to host them but also slandered them with malicious words. He then proceeded to excommunicate the members who desired to receive them. John cautioned Gaius, "Dear friend, do not imitate what is evil but what is good. Anyone who does what is good is of God. Anyone who does what is evil has not seen God" (verse 11). Diotrephes's actions were evil in that he operated in fear rather than faith. For him, the spiritual development of the church took a backseat to his desire to retain his preeminence. He did not stop to realize that favor, promotion, and recognition all come from God.

Far too many pastors live in constant fear that their members will defect to another church or that key leaders will gain too much popularity. Some pastors, in order to ensure loyalty, surround themselves with people who have few opportunities to gain any significance outside of the pastor's realm of influence. Others are so fearful of abandonment that they impose all kinds of onerous rules designed to keep congregants under control. Followers must understand the difference between servitude and servanthood. Servitude is the loss of personal freedom, while servanthood is personally choosing to serve others. When parishioners fail to understand this difference, they set themselves up for pastoral abuse. But keep this in mind: The freedom inherent in servanthood does not negate proper submission to those whom God has put over you to watch over your soul. The Holy Spirit will let you know when the relationship becomes dysfunctional. He can also give you the courage to set proper boundaries.

Insecurity is legendary among the laymen in churches. Oh, the jockeying for position, recognition, and favor with the pastor. Just watch the response of existing lay leaders and followers when new people come into the environment and express eagerness to get to work in God's kingdom. Their reaction is more likely to be subtle rejection, quiet alienation, or downright resentment rather than a warm embracing of the newcomer's skills and talents. Why is there so much contention in this area? We find the painful answer in the reality that the church is the only place where the playing field gets leveled without regard to education, social standing, or other worldly measures. Where else can a person go, who is of little significance in the eyes of the world, and achieve honor or recognition from a significant number of people? This is by no means a put-down, for the church should indeed be the place where one's pedigree and social standing are irrelevant. Many of the people Jesus associated with had no stature in their society. His disciples were common people—fishermen, for example, and even a tax collector. I believe that the church, among its other purposes, was meant to be the great equalizer. God has a place and a purpose for every person.

Even in our daily lives outside of the church walls, we must keep in mind that we are the sole heir of our destiny. No one can take it away. I witnessed this life-changing truth when I assisted a friend who was a party to a lawsuit over a contested will. The deceased had stated in his will that my friend was to be the sole heir of his estate. After numerous court appearances, the probate judge ruled in favor of my friend and granted her the property—pursuant to the deceased's will. As I reflected on the outcome of the case, I realized that each of us is the sole heir of the destiny God has willed for us. No one can thwart His plan. Of course, we may face opposition from those who attempt to, but we do so with the confidence that the victory is already ours. The Bible assures us: "For the LORD Almighty has purposed, and who can thwart him? His hand is stretched out, and who can turn it back?" (Isaiah 14:27).

If you have found yourself fearing the loss of your preeminence in a certain situation, first repent for losing your perspective on God's purpose for bringing you into such a position; that is, for His glory—not yours. Second, rest in the knowledge that God has willed your destiny; you do not have to compete for it. Finally, resist the urge to compete against others for *their* destiny. Relax and serve the Lord with joy.

Delegating

■ ■ ■ ■

You and these people who come to you will only
wear yourselves out. The work is too heavy
for you; you cannot handle it alone.

EXODUS 18:18

Moses was approaching a major burnout and didn't even see it coming. He had successfully led the children of Israel out of Egyptian bondage and now faced the inevitable task of managing the "people problem." He was fully committed to getting them to the Promised Land, and he cared about each person and their issues. Each day he sat from morning until evening functioning as the "Dear Abby" of the desert, mediating conflicts, listening to the peoples' problems, and instructing them in God's laws. Moses was weary of the long line, and the people were impatient with the pace at which it moved. Enter Jethro, Moses's father-in-law. Jethro immediately recognized that Moses's upside-down pyramid structure, with him on the bottom trying to bear up under all of the problems of his people pressing down on top, was not good for him or the people. He warned Moses that he was heading for a burnout. He suggested a plan for delegating some of the counseling tasks to a hierarchy of assistant judges, only this time with Moses sitting on top of a righted pyramid, handling only those problems that worked their way upward through the chain of command. He concluded his recommendation by saying, "If you do this and God so commands, you will be able to stand the strain, and all these people will go home satisfied" (Exodus 18:23).

Moses's response speaks volumes about his humility and his commitment to the goal of getting the job done rather than to protecting his ego and his image as the deliverer and problem-solver. It was time to let go of some of the pressure. "Moses listened to his father-in-law's advice and followed his suggestions. He chose capable men from all over Israel and appointed them as leaders over the people. He put them in charge of groups of one thousand, one hundred, fifty, and ten. These men were always available to solve the people's common disputes. They brought the major cases to Moses, but they took care of the smaller matters themselves" (Exodus 18:24-26 NLT). Smart move, Moses.

Are you effectively delegating the duties in your world of responsibilities? What about at home? If you have young children, are you assigning them age-appropriate tasks? My mother taught me how to cook for the entire family of nine when I was only seven years old. She often worked outside of the home and was sometimes bedridden from a chronic illness. She taught me how to make homemade biscuits, stuffing, and other recipes all from scratch. Of course, I was still a child and would often get creative with her food coloring. It was not uncommon for the family to sit down to red corn bread, pink potato salad, and other colorful but tasty dishes.

Are you training and delegating effectively on the job? When I worked in a high-level position at a Fortune 500 corporation, the unspoken rule was that you would not be promoted if you had not trained someone to take over your position. So whenever anyone was promoted, his first task was to identify and train his successor.

Let's look at a few reasons why some managers do not delegate:

- They have a "worker bee" mindset and do not understand the real role of management in developing their employees and directing their efforts.

- Their superegos have convinced them that they are the only ones who can do the job at their required level of perfection.

- They want to retain all authority and understand that by empowering others, they must give up some of their control.

- They feel they just do not have the time to invest in the necessary hand-holding. They fail to realize that if they make the upfront investment in the important things, they will eventually stop being victims of the urgent matters.

Now let's see if there is any hope so that, like Moses, you can learn how to improve the quality of your life by effective delegation. Here are a few delegating tips that are bound to work in your favor and decrease your stress level:

- Start with the tasks you currently perform that are basically a no-brainer for you.

- Identify someone with the capability (not just the willingness) to perform this task.

- Take the time to write out the procedures and to review them with the selected person.

- Explain why the task is necessary and its importance in the overall scheme of things.

- If the task is time sensitive, be very clear on due dates.

- Explain your other expectations.

- Finally, review the person's progress on a periodic basis until you are satisfied that he can handle the job without your intervention. This was often an area of weakness for me. My assumption was that a smart person could do anything and do it on time. I would never check on them until the due date. The results were sometimes horrible when I realized that they were not clear on the timing or objectives. I'll always remember the admonition of Bishop Frank Stewart who cautioned, "People don't do what you *expect*, but rather what you *inspect*."

Delegating should be a win-win proposition. It makes others feel empowered and valued and it frees you up to focus on more important issues and to simply have a life. I have noticed that in environments where people do not feel empowered they are more prone to working on their personal issues on company time, thus making the entire department less productive.

I believe that every manager's goal should be to assign all of his routine tasks to assistants and subordinates to the extent possible. I believe that the Jethro model still works.

Day 16

Embracing Others

The Aloof Attitude

■ ■ ■ ■

Standoffish, detached, impersonal, emotionally distant

Each of us comes into this world alone and we will leave alone. However, God never intended for any man to become an island unto himself. Shortly after He created Adam, God acknowledged that His work was not yet complete. "The LORD God said, 'It is not good for the man to be alone. I will make a helper suitable for him'" (Genesis 2:18). So He created Eve.

While some like to cite this passage to convince single men to get married, the reality is that regardless of our gender or marital status, we were all created to be in meaningful relationships with other people. If you study the life of Jesus, you will find that He was very sociable and often attended weddings, dinners, and other social events.

The phrase "one another" appears 142 times in the New King James Version of the Bible. It is clearly God's divine plan that we connect and communicate with other people in a mutually beneficial, satisfying, and productive way. To behave otherwise is counter to God's purpose for His creation. And it is our responsibility to take the initiative in connecting with others. "A man who has friends must himself be friendly" (Proverbs 18:24 NKJV).

To be aloof or emotionally detached is detrimental not only to your personal life but also to your career or business. In some professions, an aloof attitude can spell the death of a relationship. Have you ever been to a doctor or other medical service provider who treated you with cold indifference? Were you eager to see him again? What judgments did you make about him?

And what about emotionally distant people who provide other services? I was shopping at a store recently and the clerk was very aloof despite my attempts to draw her out with small talk. Knowing there were other vendors in the area who sold similar products, I silently vowed to strike that store off my list for future shopping. Rest assured, when you are aloof, people are likely making judgments about you.

Now before I get my rope to hang every aloof person I've ever met, I confess that at times I have pretended to be aloof to avoid having people engage me in conversation, such as when I've wanted to read on an airplane. I usually repented and struck up a conversation since the Holy Spirit was quick to convict me for not taking advantage of an opportunity to talk about the Lord and the status of the person's soul.

Perhaps, for reasons that you justify, you have found yourself putting emotional distance between yourself and others. What were you trying to avoid or protect yourself from? What message were you sending that you didn't have the courage to communicate with words?

As with most negative social behavior, aloofness is learned in childhood. An aloof person may have experienced a range of negativity in her family of origin or at the hands of unwise teachers, authority figures, or mean classmates. Such experiences include moving frequently to different schools or cities; abandonment; cold and emotionally detached parents; being bullied, teased, or ridiculed; and other negative interactions. All of these experiences shouted, "Connecting with people is painful!" Nevertheless, God does not want us to write off the human race as "unsafe"; rather He wants us to continue to seek connection with others. Once you begin to open up to safe people, the imbalance in your emotions toward aloofness will begin to shift.

Lest I oversimplify the solution to this problem, let me caution that a strong resolution to change is not enough. You need God's help. Luke 8:27-39 gives an account of a socially and spiritually disconnected man who was possessed by many demons. He was homeless, naked, and lived in a cemetery outside the town. Obviously, he did not engage in normal human interactions. But after his encounter with Jesus, who cast the demons out of him, he was ready to connect.

The man from whom the demons had gone out begged to go with him, but Jesus sent him away, saying, "Return home and tell how much God has done for you." So the man went away and told all over town how much Jesus had done for him (Luke 8:38-39).

I am not saying that aloofness comes from the influence of an evil spirit; rather it is an emotional handicap that can be healed by our Lord.

Once you've sought God's help, put your faith in action by joining a small study group at your church or a support group. If you have been out of the social loop at your job, why not ask a few coworkers if you may join them as they head for lunch? Do you really think they'll say no? Listen to and chime in on various discussions. Share your knowledge and don't think that you have to agree with everybody's opinion to be accepted. Have the courage to say, "I have another perspective." Even if you have nothing to contribute, ask questions that show your interest. Resist the spirit of fear when it tells you to retreat into your shell or to avoid the intimacy of a small setting.

Stay the course. God wants you connected.

The Condescending Attitude

■ ▨ ■ ▨

Behaving in a patronizing or superior manner to others

"So easy, even a caveman can do it!"

GEICO, the American auto insurance company, popularized this phrase with its humorous TV commercials that poke fun at the stupidity of cavemen trying to assimilate into modern culture. It seems that everyone has jumped on the bandwagon and uses it to convey the message, "You're an idiot if you don't get it." While the ads cause us to chuckle, a condescending attitude is no laughing matter; it hurts people. It cuts to the heart of a person's self-esteem, especially if that person tends to be insecure. Of course, most condescending people are battling their own insecurities.

When you behave in a socially or intellectually superior manner to others, it shows lack of respect, grace, and finesse. Most people with a condescending attitude do possess great knowledge and skills; however, they sabotage their success and relationships by their ignorance of basic people skills. I've observed that the downside to being brilliant is that it is often accompanied by impatience with the "slow-thinking moron," which seems to be just about the entire population in the eyes of those blessed with high intelligence and quick wit.

The apostle Paul, being a learned man himself, knew the pitfalls of having an abundance of knowledge and a rich heritage. He cautioned, "For who makes you different from anyone else? What do you have that you did not receive? And if you did receive it, why do you boast as though you did not?" (1 Corinthians 4:7). Such a person would do well to realize that his intellect, experience, and exposure are gifts from God. Paul addressed this issue further when he admonished, "Live in harmony with one another. Do not be proud, but be willing to associate with people of low position. Do not be conceited" (Romans 12:16). The charge here is to learn how to condescend without being condescending.

Let's look at some commonly used expressions in everyday personal or professional interactions that could be perceived as condescending and how to modify them so that you encourage rather than discourage effective communication.

"Let me make this simple." I have the wonderful privilege as a certified public accountant of serving as the financial consultant to a select number of churches. In presenting the sometimes technical information to their boards of directors or other groups of non-technically oriented individuals, I have to be on guard against using a phrase such as "Let me see if I can make this easy." Certainly my goal is to make the information as easy to understand as possible, but having studied human behavior for many years, I'm aware that such a statement could be interpreted as, "You are intellectually inferior and need mental training wheels to grasp this." A better phrase would be, "Please let me know if I'm not being clear enough on this point."

"That's already on the table." In brainstorming sessions duplicate ideas may be put forth as some people may be so preoccupied with trying to come up with an idea they may not have heard the original suggestion. Don't respond to person X's idea by saying, "We've already thought of

that." She could easily interpret that as "You're on the late freight. We're faster thinkers than you." Rather, say, "Thanks, great minds work alike. We're already considering that approach."

"Been there, done that!" When a friend or colleague attempts to share a helpful experience or a suggestion that you've already tried, don't just dismiss it by a curt and impersonal "Been there, done that!" as I see many people do. That's the same as saying "Useless idea!" Simply say, "Thanks for your input."

If you realize after the fact that you made a condescending remark, apologize quickly and explain what your objective was and what you should have said. "I'm sorry, I sounded condescending and I didn't mean to be. I'm really just trying to bring clarity to our discussion and to make sure that we are all on the same page."

Being sensitive to the impact that your condescending remarks can have on another requires prayer and practice. Once again, the Golden Rule should be your guiding principle. Think how you would feel if someone were to say or do to you what you are about to say or do.

The Selfish Attitude

■ ■ ■ ■

Tendency to focus on one's own needs and
interests rather than those of others

"You deserve a break today."
"Look out for Number One."
"What's in it for me?"

These popular expressions represent the attitude of our age. How did we get to the point where we are so focused on self-gratification, self-improvement, self-enlightenment, self-indulgence, and other areas with self at the center, while fewer and fewer are concerned with the needs and well-being of others?

Granted we were all born in sin and therefore have some inherent self-centeredness. However, we were also *taught* to be selfish. Now, who was the culprit, the *teacher* in your life? Was it the workaholic or absentee parent who set few spending or other limits on you because he or she felt guilty for not spending time with you? The indulgent parents who wanted to make sure you experienced every privilege that was denied them during their childhood? The absence of selfless role models? Or was it a post-childhood event, such as a deep emotional hurt that left you reeling, and you resolved to never love so selflessly again?

Or perhaps you are so overwhelmed with your own day-to-day survival that you have no energy left to think about anyone else's needs? The causes of selfishness are endless; however, they do not justify our being the central focus of our lives. God expects each of His children to deny themselves and to devote their lives to unselfish service to others.

Consider a man I'll call Roy. Though he claims to be a child of God, he is one of the most selfish people I have ever met. Practically every activity in which he engages is for his own benefit. He's always thinking of how much mileage he can squeeze out of any rare act of kindness; stacking up favors that he can call in later when he needs something. Deny himself? Never!

Who enabled him to become so selfish? A host of well-meaning siblings who decided that he was special because he was the youngest of the brood—coupled with a few desperate girlfriends who couldn't resist his charm. Ask him to sacrifice a minute of his time, even for his elderly mother, and he will give you a list of excuses a mile long. His selfishness is entrenched. Oddly enough, he always has a pressing need. Selfishness keeps you trapped in lack; nothing comes into a closed hand.

Selfishness dies hard, but it is a stronghold that we must break to experience the peace and joy that give life meaning. We're going to need a lot of support to counter this negative attitude because our justifications for being the way we are will sabotage our desire to change. Here's the plan:

- Be accountable to someone and give him permission to monitor your progress.

- Look for an opportunity to share your time or talent with a worthy cause. You need to get up close and personal so that you can empathize with the plight of others.

I had only a remote awareness of abject poverty in America until I went on a field trip to the Appalachian Mountains with World Vision USA, the Christian humanitarian organization. There I met women who told us how they had prayed for something as basic as a mop to clean their floors—right in America, the land of plenty. It broke my heart. The impact would not have been the same if I had simply read about them and sent a donation. Seeing a need firsthand nurtures your empathy and sparks a spirit of generosity.

Give away something that you really like and would prefer to keep. (This is a good challenge for your children also.) Your goal is to begin to break your emotional attachment to stuff each day. Don't keep storing up more and more for yourself. Remember the tragic end of the rich farmer Jesus told about in His parable (see Luke 12:16-21) who did not consider sharing his overflowing harvest with others but rather boasted that he would simply build bigger barns and eat, drink, and be merry. God took his life that same day.

Graduate to anonymous benevolence. Leave a needy person, such as a senior citizen, student, or single parent, a cash gift in an envelope. Do not put your name on it and do not tell anyone you did so. No, you can't deduct this on your income tax return, but God promises to return it so you can expect Him to do so in due season. "Whoever is kind to the poor lends to the LORD, and he will reward them for what they have done" (Proverbs 19:17).

B.C. Forbes, founder of *Forbes* magazine, said about selfishness, "I've never known any human being, high or humble, who ever regretted, when nearing life's end, having done kindly deeds. But I have known more than one millionaire who became haunted by the realization that they had led selfish lives."

Let me caution that this call to selflessness is not a call to abandon your self-care. You must be on guard against sacrificing for others to the point where you not only jeopardize your health and mental well-being, but become resentful for doing so. This is not God's best. Saying no may occasionally be the appropriate response to a request. The important thing is to make the decision out of a pure heart of love and wisdom.

Day 17

Stinking Thinking

The Entitlement Attitude

■ ■ ■ ■

*Believing one has a right to certain
benefits or advantages from others*

"Why didn't you repay your mother for the car loan?" Judge Judy, the popular judge on *The People's Court* television show, quizzed the young defendant.

"Because I received a grant and she didn't have to pay my tuition as planned, so I shouldn't have to pay her the money for the car. After all, she was going to be out the money anyway if she had paid my tuition."

As viewers expected, Judge Judy gave the young lady a well-deserved tongue lashing for her entitlement attitude. Such a mindset is rampant not only among the younger generation but it is pervasive in every institution of society: corporations, government, churches, schools, families, and friendships.

Some of my close acquaintances feel entitled to my time and are annoyed when I have to schedule or put time constraints on our social gatherings. Relatives feel entitled to a personal loan or gifts from me because they assume I have the money. When I managed a staff at a large corporation, they felt entitled to Christmas gifts from me simply because I was the boss and had started the practice my first year on the job. Crown Financial Ministries calls this the U-Owe-Me versus the IOU mindset.

The common attitude today is "somebody owes me something." Many Americans think that a lifetime job with good pay and a guaranteed retirement plan at 65 come with just being born, promotion is a matter of time, 40 hours a week is the maximum endurance for any worker, the last hour of each day is there to make the transition to home easier, a ten-minute coffee break should take at least half an hour, a half-hour lunch should take at least an hour and a half, and an equal share of company profits belong to the workers.

Before passing judgment on those who think this way, I took an inventory of my own entitlement attitude. Here are just a few of my entitlement rights that came to mind:

I feel entitled to a prompt response from any of my six brothers to any reasonable request I make of them because I am always there for them no matter what. Plus, I'm their only sister.

I feel entitled to a card, phone call, or some form of acknowledgement from my closest friends and family members on my birthday because I acknowledge theirs.

I feel entitled to flowers from my church if I am hospitalized because of the sacrificial giving and service I have rendered (and yes, I understand that I gave to God and not to man).

I confess that in the past I have been disappointed, frustrated, or angered in all of the instances above. As I thought about each one, I realized I had elevated each *expectation* to the status of a *right*. But what gives me—or you—such a sense of entitlement? The source of the attitude is found right in the middle of the word *entitlement* itself: "title." We think that people owe us because of the *title* we hold in their lives: mother, daughter, brother, wife, friend, donor, pastor, employee, boss. We treat that title as if it were a title deed that gives us the right to whatever benefit we expect.

Some attitudes of entitlement stem not just from personal relationship titles but also from a person's status in the culture (for example, a woman feeling that a man *owes* her his seat on a crowded train) or from past inequities ("I deserve to be taken care of by the government because of past discrimination."). When people think they have a right to such benefits, they are often ungrateful to their benefactors even when they accommodate those expectations. Have you ever extended a courtesy only to have the recipient act as if you should have done so?

I'm pleased each time I read the parable of the prodigal son and how he did not exhibit an attitude of entitlement. He left home and spent his entire inheritance—which he had insisted his father give him—on partying and fast living. An economic downturn and the resulting famine forced him to face reality; "no one gave him anything" (Luke 15:16). He returned home and said to his father, "I am no longer worthy to be called your son; make me like one of your hired servants" (Luke 15:19). He felt no entitlement to resume the good life simply because he had the title of "son." His father owed him nothing.

If you have an attitude of entitlement, here are some strategies to help you overcome this relationship-destroying mindset:

- Put each of your expectations in perspective. Ask yourself, "Is what I expect simply a *desire* or a covenantal, contractual, or constitutional *right*?" Yes, I expect fidelity from my husband as part of our marriage covenant. While I also expect him to pick up heavy objects for me, I'm very clear that this is a demonstration of his love and not a covenantal right.

- Resist the role that selfishness plays in this attitude by being willing to meet the reasonable expectations of those on whom you place expectations. Remember that meeting expectations should be a two-way street.

- Don't manipulate others into meeting your expectations by making extreme sacrifices for them and then expecting them to jump at your beck and call because of it.

- Do not assume that a person's past kindness or benevolence to you sets a pattern or entitles you to ongoing benefits. Understand that he has the freedom to eliminate or delay such a practice at his discretion.

- Make it a habit to express appreciation for every act of kindness that anyone extends to you. This will serve to remind you that nobody owes you anything!

The Racist Attitude

■ ■ ■ ■

A prejudicial and discriminatory mindset
toward a group based upon race

Racism remains a sensitive subject. It is the proverbial elephant in the room that most would prefer not to discuss. Unfortunately, the "room" is society in general. And though great strides have been made over the past decades, the elephant didn't leave the room even when the United States inaugurated its first African-American president in 2009.

Whether it was Miriam and Aaron's criticism of Moses for marrying an Ethiopian (Numbers 12:1) or the bitter relationship between the Jews and the Samaritans (John 4:9), racism has been the scourge of mankind almost since the beginning. It seems odd that this is the case—especially among Christians—since the Bible clearly states that God made all mankind in His own image and likeness (Genesis 1:26). Thus, there really is only one race—the human race. Now if God in His infinite wisdom decided that each ethnicity within the human race should have its own distinguishing features, such as skin color, hair texture, and so forth, who are we to decide that those features make one race superior or inferior to another? Anyone who has a beef with such things really has a beef with God the Creator and is guilty of rejecting His handiwork.

Perhaps you have a racist attitude because you had a negative experience with a person of another ethnicity. Are you really going to color an entire race with the actions of one ungodly person or a small group?

Many years ago my husband ordered a slice of his favorite cake at a restaurant. When he attempted to eat it with the same fork he had used to eat his fish entrée, he became nauseated. It was such a negative experience for him, he refused to eat fish for over 15 years. He hated it because he always associated it with nausea. I would often joke with him that I found it odd that he did not stop having dessert nor did he stop using forks! As he became more health conscious, he realized the benefits of eating fish, so he decided to give fish another chance. At first, he could stand to eat only fried fish or a specific type of fish. Later, he went beyond his comfort zone and experimented with a variety of fish entrées until he was finally able to enjoy the taste and benefits of fish prepared in different ways.

You may have to take this same approach if you are plagued with a racist attitude and desire to overcome it. Yes, a negative experience may have left a bad taste in your mouth. However, you're going to have to be proactive and to understand the spiritual and emotional freedom of having the right attitude toward all of God's creation.

Emotions follow behavior. If you start behaving differently toward people that you historically despised, your feelings are sure to change. Try these strategies when interacting with a particular ethnic group and you may find your disdain turning into acceptance:

- Memorize Galatians 3:28: "There is no longer Jew or Gentile, slave or free, male and female. For you are *all* one in Christ Jesus" (emphasis added).

- Smile genuinely and ask God to flow His love through you.

- Be the first to say hello.

- Engage in a conversation; remember that you really do share the same concerns, such as finances, family, and health.

- Invite someone to join you in a social activity or Bible study.

A young black couple shared with me recently that they feel isolated in their white church because those around them do not reach out to them. I challenged them to take the initiative and reach out first—and if that didn't yield the desired response, to move on to another target. Many whites are often afraid their well-meaning efforts will be rejected or misunderstood. Some simply do not know how to relate to blacks or other minorities because they have been programmed since childhood to hold certain beliefs. So they remain in their shell. The understanding and the tearing down of the walls of racism must begin with spiritually mature and courageous people—those who are filled with and controlled by the Holy Spirit.

Research the biographies of people of the disdained race who have made great contributions to society or have sacrificed for great causes—and do not conclude they were merely an exception to your biased thinking.

If you are a black person who resents white people and refuses to forgive the racial atrocities and inequities of the past, consider the many whites who marched alongside Dr. Martin Luther King, Jr. in the struggle for equality for blacks. They risked their lives, were incarcerated, were rejected by many fellow whites, and endured much suffering. Yet they marched. In his famous "I Have a Dream" speech, Dr. King paid tribute to them. "The marvelous new militancy which has engulfed the Negro community must not lead us to a distrust of all white people, for many of our white brothers, as evidenced by their presence here today, have come to realize that their destiny is tied up with our destiny. And they have come to realize that their freedom is inextricably bound to our freedom. We cannot walk alone."

Repent and ask God to forgive you and to rid you of the insidious attitude of racism. Constantly rehearsing the ills and inequities you may have suffered at the hands of a person of another race will only reinforce your negativity and hinder you from reaching your destiny.

The Haughty Attitude

■ ■ ■ ■

*Having an exaggerated opinion of
personal worth or abilities*

As I headed to the parking lot, I mused, "Today I'll finally get my opportunity to shine." After years of doing the detailed analyses, "what-if" scenarios, and other grunt work with little or no recognition, I had finally been invited by senior management to the venture capital financing meeting with our co-investors. The deal was complicated, and I knew that I understood it better than my male associates, which I was certain was the reason I was invited.

I personally made copies of the presentation to guard against any potential collating glitches by my assistant and carefully placed them in my computer bag. I checked my appearance in the office mirror. I wore a professional, cream-colored silk suit I was able to button with ease and great pride since I'd just come off my latest crash diet—down 15 pounds!

Now our investment partners will see who the real brain behind these deals is, I thought. I was overwhelmed with excitement—and pride.

As I backed out of the parking stall, I felt my tires roll over something.

When I stopped to check what had happened, to my dismay I discovered that I had left my computer bag behind the car and had backed over it! The bag was crushed almost completely flat. While the computer miraculously remained intact, the crumpled papers now resembled tostada bowls. In my effort to collect the contents of the bag, I got tire grime all over my suit. There was no time left to do anything except get to the meeting. By the time I arrived, I was so humiliated I selected a chair in a remote corner of the room and hardly said anything the entire meeting. I had gone from haughtiness to humility in three minutes.

This incident happened over 20 years ago, and I'll never forget the lesson I learned: "Pride goes before destruction, a haughty spirit before a fall" (Proverbs 16:18).

Since then, I have seared John 15:5 into my mind and spirit: "I am the vine; you are the branches. If you remain in me and I in you, you will bear much fruit; *apart from me you can do nothing*" (emphasis added). I remind myself of this every time I undertake any endeavor. I believe it with all my heart. It keeps me emotionally grounded and spiritually balanced. I have no reason to feel inadequate, nor am I tempted to become cocky with self-confidence.

Of all the destructive attitudes one could possess, haughtiness is among the worst. Why? Because God hates it (Proverbs 6:16-17). It robs Him of His glory when we attempt to take credit for what we could not have done without Him—which is everything.

What is the object of your pride? Is it your possessions? Your place in society? Your position on your job? Your profits from your profession? Do you really believe you got these things on your own? "For who makes you different from anyone else? What do you have that you did not receive? And if you did receive it, why do you boast as though you did not?" (1 Corinthians 4:7).

Once you commit to ridding haughtiness from your life, use the strategies below to jumpstart your efforts:

Ask the Holy Spirit to change your fundamental beliefs about who you are and what you can do. Meditate on the aforementioned Scriptures and allow them to become part of your spiritual fiber.

In conversation, focus your attention on the interest of others and speak less of yourself.

Respect the inherent value of every human being without regard to his social status, race, gender, or other distinguishing factors. When I met Pastor Rick Warren (author of *The Purpose Driven Life*) several years ago, I was immediately impressed with his humility. Despite the line of people waiting to talk to him, he gave me a big hug, willingly took a picture with me, and, at my request, prayed a quick blessing over my book *30 Days to Taming Your Tongue.*

And what, you may ask, is it going to buy you once you start to walk in humility? Here are the rewards:

Love and admiration. Haughtiness and pride repel, but people love and admire those who demonstrate humility. It is the most admired character trait in the world.

Personal peace. Those who have humbled themselves and submitted to their God-ordained destiny have nothing to prove—no anxiety surrounds the protection of their ego or image.

Trust and respect. Because humble people look out for the good of others, people respect their input and decisions and do not suspect them of selfish motives.

Day 18

The Power of Contentment

Enjoying Success

■ ■ ■ ■

*It is not that we think we are qualified to do anything
on our own. Our qualification comes from God.*

2 CORINTHIANS 3:5 NLT

Do you find it difficult to embrace and enjoy your success? Do you sometimes downplay or minimize your accomplishments or blessings in order to avoid provoking envy in others? Did you know you do *not* have to be emotionally secure to become successful? In fact, insecurity is often the catalyst that drives many to achieve. Their success becomes the antidote that diverts attention away from whatever it is that causes them to feel inadequate. Many high achievers succeed out of fear of poverty, fear of repeating a parent's fate, fear of disappointing the expectations of family or friends, or an endless list of other fears. Fear of success probably derails as many dreams as the fear of failure. Let's look at a few of the common concerns.

Fear of isolation. From first grade to high school, I was blessed to make excellent grades. While I enjoyed the praises of my teachers, the fear of being isolated by my peers always cast a shadow on my accomplishments. In my environment, the price one paid for excelling academically was often alienation and rejection. For me, being an extremely sociable person, this was the ultimate punishment. I made sure I always downplayed my achievements and was careful to maintain relationships with a significant number of low achievers. The same fear lurked in my mind when I

145

accomplished anything as an adult. I knew success could be alienating, so I tried to act as if I was never really that excited about anything I had done that garnered recognition or praise.

Fear of attracting insincere people. Your success will draw many people who will get their self-worth from saying that they have a relationship with you. King Solomon said, "Wealth attracts many friends" (Proverbs 19:4). It is important with each level of success to make every effort to continue to embrace your *real* friends, even though you may have outpaced them socially and financially. Share with them your sincere desire to stay connected. Prove it by including them where possible in some of your upscale activities and, most of all, by making time to do some of the things you used to do together. Refuse to be the center of attention in your conversations; focus on things that interest them.

Fear of being bombarded with financial requests. This fear is probably one of the most likely to come to fruition. I notice that many celebrities cannot enjoy an outing, even at church, without someone handing them a proposal or trying to gain favor. Of course, we understand that "for everyone to whom much is given, from him much will be required" (Luke 12:48 NKJV). Success and wealth do indeed carry a heavy responsibility— but not to every Tom, Dick, and Harry who has "the idea of the century." No one should have to live like a hermit to have a peaceful existence. It takes real emotional security to say no and not worry about the bad publicity or unpopular image you may develop as a result. You must follow your heart, give as God directs, and leave your image up to Him. Just keep in mind that God entrusts you with His money to manage for His glory.

Consider the story of John D. Rockefeller. His wealth almost proved to be his physical undoing. At 53 years old, Rockefeller earned around a million dollars a week, making him the only billionaire in the world. Unfortunately, his wealth could not cure his poor health. He was a very sick man who had to live on a boring diet of milk and crackers. Sleep eluded him as he constantly worried about his money. It seemed that Rockefeller's days were numbered. Then he discovered the secret to real success. He started pouring his money into various charitable endeavors. In turn, God poured health back into his body. He improved dramatically and lived to the ripe old age of 98. God simply wants us to enjoy His wealth His way.

Fear of envy. One of the unfortunate pitfalls of success is that many people will indeed envy your good fortune. Someone once said, "Few men have the strength to honor a friend's success without envy." It is understandable why many successful people choose to find new friends who do not make them feel guilty for having worked hard, paid their dues, and reaped the benefits of the grace and favor of God. It was not until a few years ago that I realized that favor is not necessarily fair. In fact, the essence of the word "favor" implies that one is to be preferred over another. God promised to surround His children with favor. "Surely, LORD, you bless the righteous; you surround them with your favor as with a shield" (Psalm 5:12). You cannot reject the favor God sends your way just to keep others from becoming envious.

Even though you may now be successful, you may feel that you do not deserve your good fortune or that it won't last. You may find yourself engaging in self-sabotaging behavior that will confirm your own fears and bring them to fruition. What should you do? First, thank God that you understand the root of the problem. Second, talk it out with a good listener. Talking is therapy, and it often helps to release the problem of some of its potency. You already know that your thinking is flawed. Sometimes you just need someone, not always a professional therapist, to tell you so. Happiness is a choice. You must regularly declare the words of King Solomon, "Common sense and success belong to me. Insight and strength are mine" (Proverbs 8:14 NLT).

Enjoying the Present

■ ■ ■ ■

Don't worry about tomorrow, for tomorrow will bring
its own worries. Today's trouble is enough for today.

MATTHEW 6:34

Tomorrow is like your child. No matter whom you're with or what you're doing, it tries to demand your attention. Of course, like your child, it is very important to you and you want to make sure that you take care of it. Therefore, it would be foolish and to your detriment to ignore it. It's just that every now and then, you need a break from it.

People are so distracted these days. It seems that no one knows how to enjoy the current moment or the current phase of their lives. This can cause stress as we attempt to live in two time periods at once—the present and the future. I'm working hard on being an exception to this trend. I'm practicing being present with people from the moment they come into my presence. If you are like me, one of those hard-driving, goal-oriented types, you are going to have to learn to exercise some mental discipline in order to be present with people. One of the strategies I employ is to block enough time so that I'm not thinking of what I have to do next. I find it best to wait until I can invest more than a few minutes in being with someone so that the person is not frustrated with my divided attention and my tight schedule. (Don't use this as an excuse, but as a priority in planning your schedule.) When I visit my elderly mother, I allow at least a couple of hours or more for each visit. I take her on leisurely walks aimed as much at slowing me down as they are in helping her to exercise.

Learning to enjoy the moment requires you to focus on the person or persons you are with and what they mean to you. It is helpful to ask open-ended questions that require them to respond with more than a yes or no. Listen closely and ask follow-up questions. For example, I may ask my mother, "Who was your favorite teacher in school?" followed with another question, such as a simple "Why?" This makes people feel you are being present with them and care about their responses. Sure, your thoughts may dart into the future for a few seconds, but force them back immediately by not engaging the concern. You can deal with your future issues at another time.

Be your own "in the present policeperson" when you are having a social time with your family. Do not take phone calls. Do not use this as a time to catch up on mindless work or to process your daily mail. No multitasking allowed. If you are at a wedding, block the thoughts about the report due on Monday. Silently pray for the bride and groom. Focus, focus, focus. There is great satisfaction in doing this once you get the hang of it.

I recently took my two-year-old nephew to the Long Beach pier and found great joy in watching him run freely and discover things that are old hat to me. I policed my mind and dared it not to be present with him. Of course, with a two-year-old you don't have much choice. I did not think about publishing deadlines, upcoming speaking engagements, or any of the usual suspects that pop up when I'm socializing. King Solomon cautioned, "That each of them may eat and drink, and find satisfaction in all their toil—this is the gift of God" (Ecclesiastes 3:13).

Learning to enjoy the current phase of your life is an even bigger challenge, especially as it relates to financial matters. You can become so obsessed with preparing for your future that today will have completely passed without your experiencing it. So rather than musing, fretting, and wondering about the adequacy of your retirement planning, why not hire the services (it's worth it) of a financial planner who can explain what you need to do to reach your retirement goals? Once you understand and get on track with your plan, most of the uncertainty can be eliminated, and you can focus on enjoying the now.

Mastering Your Money

■ ■ ■ ■

If you are untrustworthy about worldly wealth,
who will trust you with the true riches of heaven?

Luke 16:11

Financial friction and uncertainties are among the most frequent stressors and causes of breakdowns in relationships. Such problems are not always attributable to the fact that people do not earn enough money to cover their basic needs. As a certified public accountant, my observation has been that most people simply have not reconciled their yearnings with their earnings. My frugal father concurs. He likes to quip, "You know the best way to manage your money? Stop wanting!" The billions of dollars outstanding in consumer debt in the United States further attests to this. The masses are out of control and living in denial about their true financial status. I have heard of people who are so overwhelmed with debt that they toss their bills in the trash without even opening them.

Based upon my years of professional experience, I'd like to offer some guidelines for minimizing your financial stress:

- Spend your money according to God's priority. Pay Him His ten percent first so that you will not feel guilty about not doing so. Disobedience and guilt are real stressors.

- Pray before you buy anything. Ask yourself, "Is this a need or a want?"

- Stay aware of your level of expenditures versus your income.

- Agree with your spouse regarding the household budget as well as your short-term and long-term goals. Do not hide or miscommunicate information regarding your finances.

- Commit to being excellent at work—without overdoing your hours.

- Pay off all consumer debt (excludes real estate). Keep one credit card for identification purposes.

- Save monthly (minimum ten percent of gross pay if you are already out of consumer debt).

- Do not cosign a loan for anyone. Do not lend a relative or personal friend money you cannot afford to lose.

- Pay cash for all of your "desires." Do not charge them.

- Always allocate funds in your budget for recreation and vacations.

- When you get a raise, do not adjust your lifestyle to consume the entire amount. Practice living beneath your means.

- Establish an emergency cash reserve of at least two months' living expenses (six would be excellent).

- Be content with what you have. Do not keep striving for more, more, more. Ecclesiastes 5:10 cautions, "Whoever loves money never has enough; whoever loves wealth is never satisfied with their income. This too is meaningless."

When you know you have handled your money God's way, you can relax and expect God to show Himself strong in your life. "Do not be anxious about anything, but in every situation, by prayer and petition, with thanksgiving, present your requests to God. And the peace of God, which transcends all understanding, will guard your hearts and your minds in Christ Jesus" (Philippians 4:6-7).

Day 19

Jealousy

Justifying Jealousy

■ ■ ■ ■

*Anger is cruel and fury overwhelming, but
who can stand before jealousy?*

PROVERBS 27:4

King Saul found himself in a real dilemma. David, a bold young upstart, had killed Goliath, the Philistine giant, and was gaining in popularity daily. In fact, the women were literally singing his praises.

> When the men were returning home after David had killed the Philistine, the women came out from all the towns of Israel to meet King Saul with singing and dancing, with joyful songs and with timbrels and lyres. As they danced, they sang: "Saul has slain his thousands, and David his tens of thousands." Saul was very angry; this refrain displeased him greatly. "They have credited David with tens of thousands," he thought, "but me with only thousands. What more can he get but the kingdom?" And from that time on Saul kept a close eye on David (1 Samuel 18:6-9).

Angered and humiliated by their song, King Saul embarked upon a campaign to wipe David off the face of the earth. The insecure king was relentless in his pursuit, engaging in repeated attempts to slay the innocent lad whom he now viewed as a rival to his throne (1 Samuel 18–26).

David's lifestyle became that of a fugitive as he literally ran from place to place trying to escape the wrath of Saul.

What was this gnawing emotion that fueled Saul's behavior? It was raw, unadulterated jealousy—the fear of being displaced. It consumed him like a fire. He was determined not to rest until he eliminated the threat to his kingdom.

We can learn a lot from Saul's example. When we attempt to destroy someone whom we consider to be a threat of any kind—be it professional, relational, or otherwise—we embark upon a course that will most assuredly come to a dead end as we reap the results of the negative seeds we plant. Saul did not succeed in killing David. Rather, he and all of his sons were killed in a battle with the Philistines (1 Samuel 31). David then became king of Israel according to the sovereign plan of God.

The sovereign plan of God is a factor in our lives that we must constantly remind ourselves to consider. When jealousy rears its head and tries to make us fear that we are going to be displaced in any manner or in any circumstance, we need to swat those negative thoughts with Psalm 139:16: "You saw me before I was born. Every day of my life was recorded in your book. Every moment was laid out before a single day had passed" (NLT).

Like the powerful suction of a vacuum cleaner, jealousy can pull us into its chamber. Once there, we become angry, possessive, fearful, and totally ineffective. There are two truths I try to stay keenly aware of when I sense jealousy's lure. First, God has my back. Second, no one can thwart His plan for my life.

David held the secret to avoiding the jealousy trap. He proclaimed, "LORD, you alone are my inheritance, my cup of blessing. You guard all that is mine" (Psalm 16:5 NLT). I have come to understand that when God has determined that something is mine, I have no need to guard it, to watch over it for fear it will escape. That's God's job, not mine.

"But," you may be saying, "I'm not the jealous one. How do I deal with my mate's jealousy?" If you are committed to staying in your relationship, seek to understand the root cause of your mate's fear of being displaced or abandoned. Do not make the mistake of saying, "Tough, you just need to get over your insecurity." If it were that easy, he would have done so by now. Encourage your partner to talk about his or her childhood and past relationships. Listen without being critical or judgmental. Make it clear that you have pure intentions regarding your relationship.

Further, make every effort to be accountable. It is important to voluntarily provide adequate (read: *extra*) details to an insecure person. After all, he is looking for assurance. Learn to explain your whereabouts in a casual but thorough manner. Short, one-syllable responses will only provoke more insecurity and leave the person to imagine various negative scenarios. Remember the jealous person feels too inadequate to maintain the relationship. Continue to pray for his or her healing from this debilitating mindset, but do your part not to make the problem worse with vague communication. Caution! Stay balanced in your interaction. You must also make it clear that you will not be forced into an emotional prison by having to account for every moment of the day.

Some situations may require you to exercise the kind of wisdom that could cause others to accuse you of being insecure. For example, no matter how faithful your husband is, it is probably not a good idea to allow your girlfriend to spend the weekend in your home alone with him while you are away. I know of a woman who regularly allowed her husband to take her best friend home late at night. She was devastated when she later discovered they were having an affair. Wisdom would have dictated that she accompany them—even at the risk of appearing to be insecure. Now, you may say that if an affair is going to happen, it's going to happen anyway. Just know that a wise woman does not serve her husband to another woman on a silver platter.

Is there a relational, professional, social, or other situation in which you fear being displaced? Know that no one except you and God can affect His plan for your life. He is guarding all that is yours.

Seeking Significance

■ ■ ■ ■

Let someone else praise you, and not your own
mouth; an outsider, and not your own lips.

PROVERBS 27:2

Are you emotionally trapped by your trappings? Have you surrounded yourself with things you feel others will admire? Such behavior is the norm for lots of insecure people. In many instances, they cannot even afford their investment in their trappings. To boot, depending on the extent of their insecurity, they may even be found bragging about these possessions. People who brag about their accomplishments or possessions doubt they will be accepted based on their personal value. Therefore, they feel they must divert people's attention to something or someone they'll find impressive.

Such was Haman's plight. King Ahasuerus had appointed him prime minister, making him the second most powerful man in all of Persia. He had everything a man could desire: family, friends, favor, fame, and even a fortune. His promotion to this lofty position, however, did not cure his sagging self-esteem and nagging insecurity. Boasting became the norm in his conversations—even at home with his family. Notice his end-of-the-day conversation with his wife and friends.

> Haman boasted to them about his vast wealth, his many sons, and all the ways the king had honored him and how he had elevated him above the other nobles and officials. "And that's not all," Haman added. "I'm the only person Queen Esther invited to accompany the king to the banquet she gave" (Esther 5:11-12).

Me. My. Mine. The self-absorbed Haman thrived on the recognition and power his position afforded him. I have noticed the extreme self-centeredness and self-consciousness of those who have tied their self-worth to their stuff. Like Haman, their conversations revolve only around the things that involve them. Sadly, Haman's boasting revealed his search for significance. But the story gets worse.

King Ahasuerus had ordered everyone to bow in Haman's presence. Everyone. However, when one insignificant Jew, Mordecai, refused to bow, Haman became so angry that he started to plot not only Mordecai's death but also the annihilation of all the Jews. He decided to make a special trip to the palace to get the king's permission to implement his plan. When he arrived for the meeting, he did not even get a chance to make his request. The king had a pressing matter that needed Haman's attention. As destiny would have it, Ahasuerus had not been able to sleep the night before and had decided to read some of the chronicles of events that had occurred during his 12-year reign. He read that Mordecai had actually exposed an assassination attempt on his life. The king had never expressed any appreciation to Mordecai, not even a thank-you note. Obviously a bureaucratic—but providential—blunder.

The king asked Haman what he would do for a man whom he desired to honor. Haman assumed the king was speaking of him, so he replied,

> If the king wishes to honor someone, he should bring out one of the king's own royal robes, as well as a horse that the king himself has ridden—one with a royal emblem on its head. Let the robes and the horse be handed over to one of the king's most noble officials. And let him see that the man whom the king wishes to honor is dressed in the king's robes and led through the city square on the king's horse. Have the official shout as they go, "This is what the king does for someone he wishes to honor!" (Esther 6:7-9 NLT).

In today's terms, what Haman asked for was to be seen in the king's clothes, riding in the king's car, and accompanied by the king's companion. Oh, what an honor that would be! Imagine the bragging rights these external trappings would afford him.

Ahasuerus loved this idea. "'Go at once,' the king said to Haman. 'Quick! Take the robes and my horse, and do just as you have said for Mordecai the Jew, who sits at the gate of the palace. Leave out nothing you have suggested!'" (Esther 6:10 NLT).

What? Mordecai? Haman was mortified! Imagine his humiliation as he paraded this disrespectful, defiant Jew through the city square shouting words of honor. Afterward he rushed home, dejected and disgusted. This time when he called his wife and friends together to recount the events of the day, there was no bragging about the upcoming private banquet with the king and queen. Events had taken a strange twist. They warned him that, in light of current developments, his days might be numbered.

At the private banquet that Haman had anxiously anticipated, Queen Esther made the shocking revelation of her Jewish roots. She then proceeded to tell her husband of Haman's plot to annihilate her people. The king ordered him hanged.

Oh, if only Haman had not been so insecure as to need everyone's acknowledgment and admiration. If only he had ignored Mordecai and focused on the people who had honored him. If only he had understood that he had intrinsic worth apart from his position. If only…if only.

Haman is not alone in his pursuit of significance through external trappings. While many insecure people may not resort to bragging about their possessions and associations, they often invest inordinate amounts of money in designer apparel or other trappings. They name-drop about the important people whose coattails they are riding to significance. Their sense of inadequacy is obvious to even a casual observer.

I am careful not to judge Haman too harshly, for I know that people who live in glass houses should not throw stones. Many years ago I hitched my self-worth to a really sharp two-seat convertible Mercedes-Benz. It was my dream car; however, it proved to be a nightmare with its never-ending costly repairs. I clung to it nevertheless. Finally, I sought the Lord to take the scales from my eyes and to heal me of the insecurity that was at the root of my need for this car. He answered my prayer through a ridiculously huge repair bill totaling several thousands of dollars—and an ultimatum from my husband to sell it. I sold the car to the mechanic and refused to drive a Mercedes for more than five years. I knew a Mercedes-Benz was a good investment under normal circumstances, but I believe God allowed that car to be a thorn in my finances until I got to the point where I didn't need it to validate my worth.

What about you? Do you feel you have so little intrinsic value that you must make a conscious effort to have others focus on some impressive external trapping? Must you have the king's car, the king's clothes, or the king's companions to feel significant? Do you feel less secure without them? What person, possession, or position have you merged with your sense of worth? How would you view your life apart from him or it? Ask God to give you the grace to emotionally disconnect from the need to have this person or thing and to know beyond the shadow of a doubt that you have independent, inherent value simply because He created you for a sovereign purpose.

The Scarcity Attitude

■ ■ ■ ■

Belief in a limited supply of life's resources

"How could you sabotage our businesses like that? Why would you encourage the ladies to shop the Los Angeles wholesale district when we are here offering our wares?"

This angry vendor confronted me on behalf of the entire group of clothing vendors and boy, were they upset with me!

Even though this incident happened over 25 years ago, I can remember almost every detail. I had been invited to speak at my church's annual ladies' conference on how to shop on a budget. The conference featured some of the female entrepreneurs from the congregation who sold jewelry, ladies' clothing, and other wares primarily out of their homes. Each had purchased a vendor booth for the one-day event. It didn't occur to me when I made the suggestion to shop the deeply discounted area downtown that our vendors would think their customer base consisted only of the ladies in our local congregation. According to my confronter, my recommendation was going to have a detrimental effect on their sales.

Stunned at her outburst, I remember thinking, *How shortsighted. What little faith!* (And a few other judgmental phrases.)

Several years later, Stephen Covey would write about such a mindset in his bestselling book, *The Seven Habits of Highly Effective People.* He called it a Scarcity Mentality. Covey explained, "Most people...see life as having only so much, as though there were only one pie out there. And if someone were to get a big piece of the pie, it would mean less for everybody else." He contrasted this attitude with what he called an Abundance Mentality, in which people believe there is plenty out there and enough to spare for everybody.

I've seen the Scarcity Mentality at work in every facet of human interaction, from the insecure woman who refused to share a simple cookie recipe made with a few store-bought ingredients to the budding motivational speaker who would not share the name of a supplier with a speakers group I was hosting. Evidently, she viewed all the other attendees as competitors for a scarce supply of buyers—even though no one in the group shared her target market. (I struck her name off the list for future gatherings. I had no desire to forge a relationship with such a limited thinker.)

I've seen scarcity attitudes in families—my family. Just let me praise brother X to brother Y, and Y will find some way to diminish the action of X, as if there isn't enough praise to go around.

This attitude was also evident in the early church. Diotrephes, a church leader, would not allow the apostle John or other leaders to come and speak at his church. John explained why not. "Diotrephes, who loves to be first, will not welcome us" (3 John 9). He feared the loss of his preeminence or popularity with the congregation. Could there really be a shortage of such intangibles as love, appreciation, or loyalty?

I have seen a scarcity attitude hold back many people's plans and creative ideas. Some would-be authors have abandoned their dreams to write about a particular subject because someone else has already written about it. Even in writing this book, I had to resist defeating thoughts, such as *Who needs another book on emotions?* However, I remembered the words of a well-known writing coach, "Just write *your* book. There will be an audience for *your* book."

If you struggle with a scarcity attitude in your relationships, in your profession, or other key areas of involvement, stop and consider the implications of such a mindset. It is rooted in fear and shows distrust of the awesome power of God to supply all our needs according to His great resources. It is based upon the faulty assumption that if someone else has something, you can't have it because there is only one pie and every slice that someone else gets means less is available for you. This "you win, I lose" madness must stop now. It will make you a rotten team player because you will think that sharing diminishes your portion. This is no way to live the abundant life.

Start today to reprogram your thinking. Remind yourself that you are not in competition with anybody for anything in any area of your life. Cling to the words of Jesus, "I have come that they may have life, and that they may have it to the full" (John 10:10).

Day 20

The Power of a
Positive Perspective

The Grumpy Attitude

■ ■ ■ ■

Irritable, moody, out of sorts

Ding-dong…Ding-dong…Ding-dong.

"Who in the world could that be?" I muttered.

I glanced at the clock and saw that it was only 7 a.m. I had gone to bed after 3 a.m. and had planned to sleep at least seven hours. I peeked out the window only to see the gardener standing at the front door with a sheepish look on his face. He had forgotten his key to the backyard security gate—again. I barreled downstairs, grabbed my spare key from the windowsill, and handed it to him without a word. I'm sure he thought, *Grumpy broad!* I justified my actions by concluding that grumpiness is not my usual demeanor.

Are you generally in a good mood? Do you make it a point to respond pleasantly to others most of the time? It is one thing to have an occasional incident like the one above that causes you to show irritation, but a pattern of being irritable, moody, or out of sorts is a sign that your life is out of balance. Further, those in your circle of interaction will find it difficult to relate to you—much like trying to hug a porcupine.

As with any negative behavior, the first step to overcoming it is to acknowledge the problem. Notice I didn't say *justify* the problem. Simply be truthful with yourself as you replay your most recent encounters with others. Do you need to take corrective action? Here are a few surefire strategies that will bring you into the land of the pleasant.

Pray immediately upon arising. Don't wait until you are bombarded with the stressors of the day; get God on your side first thing. Ask Him to infuse you with His peace and joy and to empower you to respond His way throughout the day. Remember, "The joy of the LORD is your strength" (Nehemiah 8:10).

Get adequate sleep. Most of us think of sleep as some passive process in which we drift off into oblivion and wake up several hours later hopefully being more rested. The truth of the matter is that sleep is a very active state. Many metabolic and other restorative processes occur during the various stages of sleep. If we do not sleep long enough for our system to be rejuvenated, we will most likely find ourselves irritated by the smallest things.

Get a medical checkup. You may be a "pain in the neck" due to a literal pain in the neck or other parts of your body. My otherwise fun-loving husband was constantly grumpy when he battled with cluster headaches. With proper medication, the excruciating attacks subsided and he returned to his normally fun self.

Exercise. Even a short period of stretching, walking, or other forms of exercise can affect your mood by raising the endorphins ("feel good" hormones) in your brain. Get outside and inhale fresh air if at all possible. Try a group exercise class for even more benefits.

Watch your diet. Too much caffeine, sugar, or refined foods will negatively affect your mood. If you must indulge, be sure to combine a "bad" snack choice with some healthy protein (cheese, turkey, nuts) to slow down the absorption of the sugar into your bloodstream and to prevent a spike in your insulin.

Say yes to requests for personal favors only when you want to. This will prevent you from becoming overloaded and resentful regarding work dumped on you by others.

Plan a social activity with positive friends. Stay away from negativity. "Do not be misled: 'Bad company corrupts good character'" (1 Corinthians 15:33).

Focus on the needs of others. There is nothing like bringing light and hope to the less fortunate to change your grumpy attitude. When I teach self-development classes at the local homeless shelter for women, I reap huge emotional dividends. It just feels like the right thing to do.

Dig deeper. If none of the above strategies help your grumpiness, look deeper into your soul and be honest about what's really irritating you. Do you need to confront an inequity? Frustrated with your lack of direction? What's really going on with you? If necessary, talk to a counselor or someone who knows you well.

The Sullen Attitude

■ ■ ■ ■

Refusal to talk, behave sociably, or cooperate cheerfully

You have encountered it in the retail clerk who barely says hello at the checkout counter, the teenager who seems to hate life in general, or the sulky employee, wife, or boyfriend who has not learned to express their preferences, dislikes, or other wishes in a productive way. It's the sullen attitude. It is a poor communication strategy and a real frustration to others.

Of course, there is nothing new under the sun. Thus, we find several biblical characters who demonstrated a sullen attitude. Consider the story of King Ahab, who could not handle that a certain landowner rejected his request to buy a plot of land from him.

> So Ahab went home, sullen and angry because Naboth the Jezreelite had said, "I will not give you the inheritance of my ancestors." He lay on his bed sulking and refused to eat. His wife Jezebel came in and asked him, "Why are you so sullen? Why won't you eat?" (1 Kings 21:4-5).

Here we have the king of Israel pouting like a baby because he can't have his way. Of course, he was a wicked king and such conduct can be expected from those who have not submitted their lives to the will and purpose of God.

And what about the attitude of the "good son" in the story of the prodigal son? The bad son wasted his entire inheritance and returned home, humble and broken. When the good son learned that his father was throwing a party in celebration of Mr. Wasteful's return, he grew sullen and refused to attend (Luke 15:28). Once again we have a grown man sulking because he doesn't like what's going on and makes no attempt to understand all the ramifications. The father explained the significance of the event, but he did not cater to his son's sullen attitude by canceling the party. Good move!

If you have resorted to eye rolling, door slamming, silent treatment, running away, or other passive-aggressive forms of communicating your displeasure, it's time to grow up. Mature people express their concerns rather than expect others to read their minds.

I'm going to cut you a little slack here because your sullen attitude may not be your fault entirely. Odds are that you learned it, which means you had a teacher...perhaps several teachers, such as weak parents, a weak spouse, a weak boss, or weak friends. I often say, we *teach* by what we *tolerate*. I have watched parents unwittingly teach their children that it was okay to exhibit a sullen attitude by tolerating it. In so doing, they created an environment of disrespect.

Call me old-fashioned, but when I was growing up, we were not allowed to be sullen. The consequences were immediate and much more severe than "Go to your room!" But that was then.

Perhaps your spouse or girlfriend may have taught you that sullenness works by catering to your pouting to avoid the discomfort of your alienation. Expressing our needs, expectations, or disappointments in a respectful way has been a cardinal rule in my marriage for over 30 years. We believe it is unfair to do otherwise. Further, a sullen attitude opens the door for resentment, that relational termite that destroys the foundation of marriage and any other relationship.

So whether or not you were "taught" that a sullen attitude gets results, it is your responsibility to conquer it. Here's how:

- Evaluate the issue from a *total* perspective versus how it is affecting you only. Your expectations may be unreasonable or you may be unaware of what it costs to meet your need. Try asking, "What factors could hinder you from granting my request?" Seek to understand. Listen intently to the response and stay calm and respectful if you feel the need to rebut it.

- Abandon your inflexible attitude and be willing to negotiate an alternative solution.

- Submit all of your desires to God with a "nevertheless...not my will but Yours" mindset.

- Understand that "No" is often God's way of achieving a higher purpose in your life. We will not always get everything we want. Working through disappointment builds character.

Maintaining a Positive Outlook

■ ■ ■ ■

Abraham never wavered in believing God's promise. In fact, his faith grew stronger, and in this he brought glory to God.

Romans 4:20 nlt

I lost the keys to my car today. I attended a luncheon in downtown Los Angeles and decided to meet my friend Yvonne at her office and ride with her. After the luncheon, I assumed that my keys were in my purse when we left the hotel. When I realized they were lost, I was particularly concerned because the car's ignition key was the type that had to be ordered from the manufacturer at an exorbitant price. I resisted the temptation to succumb to a negative attitude regarding whether or not I would get the keys back. I refused to envision myself writing the check for the replacement key. I also reminded myself that God was fully aware of the fact that I had a critical doctor's appointment in the next hour and could not be late for it. Most importantly, God knew exactly where those keys were; nothing is ever hidden from Him. After much searching, phone calls, and prayer, the hotel staff located the keys. All ended well.

This incident may pale in comparison to the challenge you are facing; however, the principle of Romans 8:28 is always the same: God works things out on our behalf when we love Him and are called according to His purpose. He is just as concerned about lost keys as He is about insufficient funds, troubled relationships, terminal illnesses, or any other of life's challenges.

Maintaining a positive outlook requires not only faith, but also mental discipline. While you may believe that God is in control of your life, oftentimes the reality of a situation can overwhelm your mind and threaten to negate your faith. In times like these, it pays to have developed the habit of "casting down arguments and every high thing that exalts itself against the knowledge of God, bringing every thought into captivity to the obedience of Christ" (2 Corinthians 10:5 NKJV). As you arrest those negative thoughts, "fix your thoughts on what is true, and honorable, and right, and pure, and lovely, and admirable. Think about things that are excellent and worthy of praise" (Philippians 4:8 NLT).

The amount of stress you experience in a situation will be determined by your attitude toward what is happening. If you start confessing that you are overwhelmed, then you will experience what you have heard, for faith comes by hearing. On the other hand, if you maintain that God is in control and that you will prevail, indeed you will. Begin to act as your own "attitude policeperson." Start to notice how you respond to long lines, undesirable weather, impossible relatives, or other would-be negative situations. Do not justify your behavior. To be associated with Christ is to be positive; it is a result of being filled with the Spirit of God. There should be no such thing as a "pessimistic Christian" any more than there is "cold hot sauce." What's in us gives us our flavor.

If you find that your attitude tends to lean toward the negative, try the following to get you on the road to a better mindset:

- Watch the company you have been keeping. Attitudes are contagious.

- Regularly read the miracles of the Bible and the exploits of men and women of faith.

- Prayerfully consider a change if your church does not adequately emphasize a life of faith.

- Know that pessimism is an insult to your omnipotent Father. It is an indication of your lack of faith in Him to make matters better.

- Consider how your attitude impacts your witness for Christ.

A positive attitude will not only minimize how much stress affects you, but also has a direct correlation to how our bodies respond to diseases. Numerous studies have shown that optimistic people who are diagnosed with terminal illness tend to live way beyond the normal predicted life span. "A peaceful heart leads to a healthy body" (Proverbs 14:30).

Day 21

Stress Less

Identifying Your Stressors

■ ■ ■ ■

Please listen and answer me, for I am
overwhelmed by my troubles.

PSALM 55:2 NLT

I have done countless analyses during my career as a financial executive; however, until a couple of years ago, I had never done a stressor analysis in which I listed the situations or people that were bringing pressure to bear upon me and evaluated the extent to which that pressure was impacting me. Stress is our biological response to the pressures of life. The pressures do not necessarily have to be negative to have a negative impact on our bodies, nor must they be the things that are the obvious. I had assumed that things that kept me the busiest would be the primary stressors, but that did not prove to be true. Here are the results of my analysis:

- Mother's housing and health care issues
- My eternal weight loss battle
- Inability to find qualified employees
- Balancing the increasing demands of my dual careers
- My husband's tentativeness about his career objectives

As I pondered my stressors, I objectively categorized them into those I could impact and those outside of my circle of influence. In addition to the major stressors, I also had minor stressors not caused by external situations, but rather by my traditional thinking and entrenched attitudes. While my mother's situation caused me the most concern, I knew that due to certain home ownership issues and her insistence on living in her familiar but problem-ridden environment, I could do very little to make an impact. Therefore, I had to develop an effective coping strategy. I have learned to segment and delay my mental preoccupation with certain situations when other stressors demand my attention. I call it "managing my sanity." God has given me the grace to do it.

My dual career was beginning to require most of my attention. I had felt for the past two years that my season was up as the chief financial officer of the church, but I just couldn't bring myself to tell my boss, even though my husband and others who were sensitive to the voice of God were pressing me to do so. I loved the bishop. He was the most endearing boss I had ever had. My experience with him was nothing like the horror stories I had heard from my counterparts in other ministries. He rarely called me at home, and if he did, he was very apologetic about it and genuinely needed something that could not wait. I worked crazy hours because I felt that he and the church deserved the same level of effort I had given to companies I had worked for in the corporate world. Notwithstanding, the work never seemed to be done. The job had taken its toll on my health. It was time to take care of myself and time to obey God.

Over a two-year period, I had no fewer than ten different highly respected Christian leaders strongly encourage me to go into full-time ministry. I did not want God to have to drag me kicking and screaming to my destiny, so I finally mustered enough courage to tender my resignation. It took five tissues for me to tell the bishop. I cried for the entire month leading up to the final date. I had worked many, many 16-hour or more days. I had even postponed a couple of needed surgeries because I could never find an extended period to be away from the office. I had not realized I was so emotionally invested in the place until I faced the reality that I would no longer be there.

We had built this awesome $66 million cathedral, and I had signed the check for every single item in it. It was featured in several popular magazines. Further, my husband and I had sacrificed and made a significant financial investment in the project. I felt a deep sense of ownership. I knew

God was saying, "Okay, mission accomplished." However, I just wanted to settle down and enjoy the fruit of my labor. Plus, I had finally become comfortable with my expertise of every aspect of our operation. It did not seem right to let it all go to waste.

Many times the path to God's perfect will for our lives requires us to make various transitions. For example, to get to San Diego, California, where I often speak, I have to travel on Interstate 10 for a few miles, transition to the 110 Freeway for several more miles, and finally transition to the 405 Freeway for more than 100 miles before I reach San Diego. Obviously, I would never get there if I remained on I-10. Transitions are sometimes mandatory if we want to achieve our ordained destiny. We are created with free will, which is not to say that God does not have a special plan for our lives, yet it is *we* who act outside God's will, therefore missing the blessings He has for us. Many times God is saying, "Time to transition to the next path." But we respond, "I'm very familiar with this route. Can't I just stay here and still reach my destiny?" Then we have the audacity to become frustrated or blame God when our goals seem to elude us.

I had to get real about my stressors, and yes, the financial consequence of the transition was weighing heavily on my mind. Being a CPA, I resisted the natural temptation to do a detailed analysis of the impact of taking my income out of the household budget. I truly wanted to make a faith decision rather than a financial one. I do not recommend this approach under normal circumstances. I simply had the personal assurance of the Holy Spirit that God was going to do exceedingly and abundantly above all that I could ask or think. Further, I knew that all of our needs would be met no matter what my husband's career decision was going to be. So I took the plunge. God has been faithful to His Word and we have not missed a beat financially.

Have you taken the time to analyze your stressors? I suggest you find a quiet place where you will not be interrupted for at least 30 minutes. Make a list of every situation stressing you. Include everything from the annoying friend who competes with you to your messy, irresponsible teenager whom you love with all your heart. Now rank each one from most to least stressful. Meditate on what God would have you do in confronting these situations. You might also want to discuss some coping strategies with a trusted friend or counselor.

Stopping the Stress Speak

■ ■ ■ ■

*You are snared by the words of your mouth; you
are taken by the words of your mouth.*

PROVERBS 6:2 NKJV

Do you realize how often you program yourself for stress by the words or phrases you use to describe simple activities that do not necessarily need to be done quickly? In this section, I want you to become sensitive to your stress-oriented vocabulary. I hope you will find alternate ways of describing your actions so that you are not snared into a stress-mode by the words of your mouth. Consider the examples below:

Stress-oriented: "I have to run to the store."
Alternative: "I'm going to the store."

Stress-oriented: "Let's grab a bite to eat."
Alternative: "Let's have lunch."

Stress-oriented: "I'm going to jump in the shower."
Alternative: "I'm going to take a shower."

Stress-oriented: "I'm going to throw the clothes in the dryer."
Alternative: "I'm going to put the clothes in the dryer."

Stress-oriented: "I'll swoop by and pick up Jane for the party."
Alternative: "I'll pick up Jane for the party."

Stress-oriented: "I'll be back in a flash."
Alternative: "I'll be back shortly."

Stress-oriented: "I'll hurry over before the game starts."
Alternative: "I'll be over before the game starts."

Stress-oriented: "I'm going to zip through this part of the report."
Alternative: "I'm going to cover this section briefly."

All of these stress-oriented phrases imply a sense of urgency that sends a message to your body to get the adrenaline pumping.

Even if we do not initiate the rush vocabulary, we are still surrounded with rush messages from all forms of the media. There is a popular television commercial that exhorts customers to "Run, don't walk!" to their upcoming sale.

You may have other phrases, in addition to the ones above, that you are in the habit of using. On your road to stressing less, why not become conscious of how you describe your activities? Catch yourself in action and start reprogramming your vocabulary.

Further, I will challenge you to try to stop using the word "stress" or "stressed out" when describing your situation. Since stress affects your mind and your body, why send an unnecessary alarm to them? If you have many pressures that are being brought to bear upon you, rather than saying, "I'm stressed out," try saying, "I am working through several projects and personal issues right now. I know that the Holy Spirit is going to help me to get through them all."

Just recently I had to complete 80 hours of continuing professional education credits within a two-week period and was also faced with a publishing deadline with the same due date. Rather than focusing on the potential stress this was sure to cause, I started looking for quick solutions. I found a few self-study courses and completed the continuing education task within a week. Further, I asked for and was granted a 30-day extension on the publishing deadline.

If you are faced with deadlines and other pressures, stay solution oriented. Most importantly, ask God for His intervention. "In all your ways acknowledge Him, and He shall direct your paths" (Proverbs 3:6 NKJV).

The Case for Laughter

■ ■ ■ ■

A merry heart does good, like medicine.

PROVERBS 17:22 NKJV

I love to laugh. Humor has been a key stress reliever for me for as long as I can remember. In fact, many people have told me they assumed I had no problems because I always seem so happy. What they do not realize is that if I thought about it for more than a minute, I could find something to cry about each day. Rather than focusing on what isn't, I've made a conscious decision to maintain a merry heart.

"I recommend having fun, because there is nothing better for people in this world than to eat, drink, and enjoy life. That way they will experience some happiness along with all the hard work God gives them" (Ecclesiastes 8:15). These words of King Solomon should be taken to heart.

The impact of laughter on stress is well documented. Studies show that laughter lowers blood pressure and reduces hypertension. It reduces stress hormones and cleanses the lungs and body tissues of accumulated stale air, because laughter empties more air out than it takes in. It boosts immune functions in the body. In addition to all these benefits, laughter triggers the release of endorphins—those "feel good" chemicals in the brain that make you feel joyful and elated. These are the same chemicals released when some people, after an extended period of running, experience a runner's high.

Being merry is an individual choice. No one can force anyone else to be merry by saying, "Just be happy!" When the Israelites were taken captive by the Babylonians because of their disobedience, they lost all desire to play their musical instruments. "We put away our harps, hanging them on the branches of poplar trees. For our captors demanded a song from us. Our tormentors insisted on a joyful hymn: 'Sing us one of those songs of Jerusalem'" (Psalm 137:2-3 NLT). Your ability to laugh and to be merry is often a good indicator of where you are in your relationship with God. The Israelites had lost their connection with God. "How can we sing the songs of the LORD while in a foreign land?" (Psalm 137:4). Your stressful lifestyle can take you so far away from God that you feel you are in a foreign place spiritually and unable to laugh and to find joy in the things that once caused you to be merry.

Humorous situations surround us each day. We just have to be on the lookout for them and not ignore them. We should take advantage of every opportunity to have a good hearty laugh. I remember one morning when Darnell and I had joined hands to pray, he began by saying, "Father, we come before your groan of thrace..." I was so overcome with laughter that I could not focus on the prayer. He would not stop to allow me to regain my composure. He just kept right on praying and I kept right on laughing.

I asked him later why he would not stop, and he replied, "I wasn't going to acknowledge the devil!" We still laugh about that incident today.

Swap jokes with friends. Let people know you enjoy a good laugh. Don't be shy about sharing your most embarrassing moments (let good taste prevail here). Laugh at your mistakes—especially on the job. Shed that Superwoman image and start having fun. This doesn't mean you have relaxed your standards for excellence. It just indicates you are aware of the fact that you and those around you are human. So have fun. Be a good sport. When others do imitations of you, laugh and pay attention. That can be a real eye-opener to some of your eccentric ways.

I should caution you to be careful in teasing others. It is not wise to have a laugh at someone else's expense by making them the butt of a joke. Some people are extremely sensitive and insecure, so make note of them and veer toward the fun people.

Don't allow life's pressures and negative circumstances to snuff out your sense of humor. Laughter reflects positive emotions and makes you a lot more fun to be around. Nobody enjoys a sourpuss. Laughter can also take your mind off of what's stressing you. Laugh often, "for the joy of the LORD is your strength!" (Nehemiah 8:10).

Day 22

Poisonous Attitudes

The Dismissive Attitude

■ ■ ■ ■

Showing arrogant, offhand disregard

As I began to write each chapter of this book, I examined myself to see if I tend to exhibit the particular attitude before I launched into "fixing" the reader. It took only a few minutes of reflection to realize that I have indeed been dismissive in certain situations. While I'll spare you the details, I will share a couple of the reasons I did so.

In one instance, the target of my dismissive attitude did not have his facts right or attempted to make an argument he could not produce any concrete evidence for. I hate it when people do that (yes, I know, you do too!). I'm determined not to argue with a fool, so I waved him off. In another instance, my target had his facts right, but I had so many stressors at the time that I didn't want to hear about my communication failure, so I dismissed his input to protect myself against the painful truth.

I've seen others adopt a dismissive approach when they have an entrenched attitude toward the issue being discussed or negative feelings about the person making the request or argument. For example, I was walking on the beach with two friends I'll call Rhonda and Sally. Rhonda remarked how much she enjoyed taking in the beauty of the California coastline at sunrise.

"Next time, you should grab your camera and capture the moment," Sally responded.

"Oh please, it's not that serious!" Rhonda said.

I felt bad that Sally's suggestion had been dismissed so insensitively. Of course Sally did have the annoying habit of always telling us what we should be doing. It was still no excuse for how Rhonda responded.

Husbands are often guilty of being dismissive of a wife's concern. This can be a real relationship buster. Consider this conversation between John and Marge when they were returning home from his company's social function.

"Betty seemed to be flirting with you at the party tonight," Marge said.

"Oh, quit being so insecure!" John replied.

John could have said, "Hmmm, I wasn't aware of it. Even so, you're the only one for me." Now how smooth is that? He'd certainly get more mileage out of this response than out of his.

If you are a supervisor or one in authority, you must also be aware of how you respond to the opinions of your subordinates as it can have a detrimental impact on morale and productivity. Even if someone puts forth an idea that you find without merit, you must resist the temptation to dismiss it on the spot. A simple "Thanks for your input" will have a greater impact than "That won't work."

Whatever the relationship, when you are dismissive toward anyone, it sends a message: "Your issue is insignificant to me," "Your feelings or opinions don't matter," "I'm disregarding you or your idea." Spoken or unspoken, these statements cut to the heart of a person's sense of value and need for respect. This is especially true if the person believes he has earned the right to special consideration.

This is demonstrated in the story of Nabal and David in 1 Samuel 25. Nabal was a very rich man who lived in a city some distance from where he sheared his sheep. During David's time of fleeing the wrath of King Saul, he and his 600 men camped near where Nabal's shepherds tended his sheep, providing a wall of protection for them. Later, when they needed food supplies, David sent a contingent to ask Nabal to help them out and to remind him of how they had protected his flock and his shepherds. Nabal responded like the fool that his name meant:

> Nabal answered David's servants, "Who is this David? Who is
> this son of Jesse? Many servants are breaking away from their

masters these days. Why should I take my bread and water, and the meat I have slaughtered for my shearers, and give it to men coming from who knows where?" (1 Samuel 25:10-11).

His dismissive attitude almost cost the lives of his entire household. When David's men told him how Nabal had responded, he ordered them to join him in wiping out everybody and everything associated with Nabal. Had it not been for the intervention of Nabal's beautiful and wise wife, Abigail, all would have been lost. She quickly prepared adequate provisions for the entire army and personally delivered them as a peace offering. She met David as he was en route to destroy Nabal, his family, and workers. David's anger was appeased.

Know that when you are dismissive toward others, many times they will find a way to show their displeasure. You could avoid a relational disaster by becoming more aware of your behavior.

Understand that opinions, needs, and ideas are as personal and individual as taste buds. Just because you don't think a certain way about a matter doesn't mean that you can be dismissive to those who act or think differently. The only solution to this problem is to step outside yourself and listen attentively and purposefully to others and make every effort to fully understand and address their concerns. You'll reap great dividends as a result.

The Critical Attitude

■ ■ ■ ■

Tendency to judge or criticize the conduct,
character, or choices of other people

When Donna entered the church sanctuary, the usher handed her a three-fold brochure that featured prayers and affirmations prepared by Pastor Joe. He was a great teacher and the information would surely prove helpful in the upcoming weeks. However, the only thing Donna could focus on was that the folded brochure opened inwardly rather than outwardly.

What incompetent fool did this? she thought as she was ushered to her seat. As soon as she sat down, she proceeded to fold the brochure correctly—the way brochures are "supposed" to be. Of course, her new fold threw the page sequence off. So she took out her pen and renumbered the pages. She made a mental note to call the church staff to prevent this from happening again.

The worship team had already begun singing the morning hymn. Donna immediately noticed the unflattering fit and inappropriate skirt lengths that some of the female team members wore. *They need to wear uniforms,* she mused. *Their appearance is distracting!*

After what Donna judged as several unnecessary, time-consuming announcements, Pastor Joe finally took the pulpit and began his message. Within minutes, the microphone started to screech and finally went silent. This was becoming a recurring annoyance on Sunday mornings. *Good Lord,* Donna thought, *when are they going to fix that sound system?*

The service ended and Donna left feeling the entire endeavor had been one big waste of time. Despite the life-changing principles Pastor Joe had taught, she had felt no connection to God that day. Even though she had not verbalized her observations to anyone, Donna's faultfinding had sabotaged her experience.

I can relate to Donna for I have a tendency to judge other people's poor choices, shortcomings, and inefficiencies. It just seems hard to overlook behavior that doesn't line up with what I think reflects excellence or what "should" be. I'm on a campaign to banish this attitude from my life.

A critical attitude has at least three negative consequences.

First of all, it is a sin. When Aaron and Miriam, Moses's brother and sister, criticized him for marrying an Ethiopian woman, God judged them by striking Miriam with leprosy, the dreaded disease of the day that immediately made her a social outcast. Aaron was quick to repent. "He said to Moses, 'Please, my lord, I ask you not to hold against us the sin we have so foolishly committed'" (Numbers 12:11). Moses prayed that God would heal Miriam, and God immediately answered his prayer.

Second, our sin of a critical attitude can isolate us from cherished relationships. Even after Miriam was healed of leprosy, the Lord decreed that she should be "in disgrace for seven days" (Numbers 12:14). She was shut outside the camp, away from all human companionship. The laws regarding lepers required this separation. A critical spirit is relational leprosy, and we may find people treating us accordingly.

When my 11-year-old niece sent me an email, I was delighted; however, it contained several spelling and grammatical errors. I took the liberty of correcting each one and sending her the corrections. I told her that I wanted to turn our emails into a learning experience for her. I haven't received another email from her since! I'm not naïve as to why this may be so. People embrace those who accept them "as is," for no one enjoys being under the constant eye of a critic. This doesn't mean that we never give constructive feedback. However, we need to lean more toward affirmation and encouragement and to address only matters of serious concern.

Third, a critical attitude hinders our progress and that of others in our circle of interaction. Miriam's isolation brought the entire pilgrimage to the Promised Land to a temporary halt. "So Miriam was confined outside the camp for seven days, and the people did not move on till she was brought back" (Numbers 12:15).

Have you ever been a part of an organization where one faultfinding person destroyed the effectiveness or progress of the entire group? Or what about the critical parent or spouse who so destroys the confidence of a child or mate that he or she never develops the coping or survival skills to move forward in life?

If that critical person is you, let's see if we can identify the root cause of your behavior and how you can eliminate it from your life. What makes us critical? A critical spirit is learned behavior. Here are a few of the reasons why some have such a spirit:

Many critical people were raised by parents or others who had no clue how to affirm another person—so they never saw affirmation modeled. Some parents erroneously believe that being critical inspires a child to achieve great success.

Sometimes, because of our unique gifting or experience, we don't stop to consider that our talents and experience are indeed unique to us—and given by the grace of God. Thus, we unwisely expect everyone else to measure up to our level.

Pride and arrogance because of past successes can also cause us to think that we know what is best for all; down with the "idiots" who do not do things "our" way.

Our unresolved anger and hurt over past incidents (or just plain envy) can cause us to harbor resentment toward some people and to use every opportunity to diminish their image in the eyes of others.

Finally, a critical spirit is often an unconscious attempt to hide our own faults and shortcomings by casting a negative light on others. I challenge you to stop now and think of the person, group, or organization you are most critical of and consider whom you criticize them to. Are you trying to increase your stature in the eyes of others?

The Cure

Know what God's Word says about a critical spirit: "Do not judge, or you too will be judged. For in the same way you judge others, you will be judged, and with the measure you use, it will be measured to you" (Matthew 7:1-2). Do you really want to reap the consequences of planting such a negative seed?

Acknowledge and repent of the sin of judging or faultfinding. If this is a habit in your family, determine that by the power of the Holy Spirit, the trend stops with you.

Look for admirable qualities in those you criticize, especially qualities you may not possess. I once had a client who had an incompetent employee whose performance I always found myself criticizing. When I started to look for his good qualities, I realized that he had a teachable spirit and readily admitted his mistakes—versus my tendency to rationalize away my mistakes or to blame others. I also pondered if I was unconsciously trying to enhance my image as "Superwoman" in the client's eyes.

Commit to extending to others the grace and mercy God extends to you daily. "Blessed are the merciful, for they will be shown mercy" (Matthew 5:7).

The Controlling Attitude

■ ■ ■ ■

*Demanding; attempting to manipulate
the behavior and choices of others*

Rare is the person who will readily admit to having a controlling attitude. We all know it's a toxic mindset and would prefer to give this behavior a more socially acceptable label, such as perfectionism, determination, or strong personality. Rather than force a confession from you, I'm going to ask you to take a quick quiz. Simply "tell the truth and shame the devil" (as my elders used to say), and you'll be on the road to healing in no time.

Do you become moody or irritated when people don't do what you want them to do?

Do you blame others when your mistakes are pointed out?

Do you generally cause stress for other people by forcing them to comply with your perfectionism or to work faster or longer?

Have you ever pretended to be emotionally distressed, sick, or suicidal in order to manipulate someone's decision or to gain his attention or sympathy?

Do you criticize the opinions or choices of others and thereby position yourself as superior?

Do you become perturbed or even abusive (verbally or physically) when someone disagrees with you or challenges your authority?

Are you reluctant to compliment others and instead find yourself "fixing" something "wrong" with them?

Would you find it hard to say to someone, "I need you"?

Do you try to cause trouble or create distance between your spouse, friend, relative, or coworker and someone who loves or supports them?

Do you bark commands at employees, waiters, friends, your spouse, or others and omit social niceties such as "please" and "thank you"?

While I'm no psychologist and this is not a scientific test, I think you can render your own verdict about your behavior. Even if you answered yes to only a couple of these questions, you are probably battling a controlling attitude. Have you ever stopped to consider how your behavior is affecting others? If not, let me give you a glimpse. Here is an excerpt of an email I received just today from a woman who had reached the end of her rope with her controlling friend:

> My friend and I stayed at a motel for an out-of-town Bible conference. We were assigned a non-smoking room; however, she smoked anyway. She is very forceful and controlling. I should have spoken up, but I didn't. The motel fined me $150. Further, during the weekend, my friend told me how and when to do just about everything. I held my tongue because I did not want to argue with her. Whenever I try to express my disagreements with her, she gets very upset. I seem to have a hard time drawing a line here. Help!

As I reread the email, key words jumped out: "she is very forceful"; "I seem to have a hard time drawing a line here." Little did the writer know she had revealed the solution to her problem, for herein is the secret to the controller's success: people are afraid to draw the line with them, to set and enforce relational boundaries. Therefore, like a bulldozer, controllers by the sheer force of their personality or the power of their position steamroll right over people who find it easier to submit to their domination and manipulation rather than face their wrath.

Ironically, people who are controlling are scared stiff of losing control. Relationship expert Joshua Uebergang explains,

> To them, it's easier to go the route of controlling people instead of dealing with people from a level of self-respect and dignity. To them, having a controlling attitude saves energy and time. These people have visions of acting like an all-powerful God with an overruling dominance over the lives of others. Life to them is no sweat when giving the commands rather than receiving them.

Jezebel, the wicked wife of Ahab king of Israel, was the consummate controller. As we saw earlier, Ahab wanted to purchase a vineyard adjacent to the palace so that he could have a vegetable garden. However, Naboth, the landowner, refused to sell it to him. When Ahab related the story to Jezebel, she showed total disregard for Naboth's decision. She devised a plot to falsely accuse Naboth of wrongdoing and to have him stoned to death.

> Jezebel his wife said, "Is this how you act as king over Israel? Get up and eat! Cheer up. I'll get you the vineyard of Naboth the Jezreelite." So she wrote letters in Ahab's name, placed his seal on them, and sent them to the elders and nobles who lived in Naboth's city with him. In those letters she wrote: "Proclaim a day of fasting and seat Naboth in a prominent place among the people. But seat two scoundrels opposite him and have them bring charges that he has cursed both God and the king. Then take him out and stone him to death." So the elders and nobles who lived in Naboth's city did as Jezebel directed in the letters she had written to them...As soon as Jezebel heard that Naboth had been stoned to death, she

said to Ahab, "Get up and take possession of the vineyard of Naboth the Jezreelite that he refused to sell you. He is no longer alive, but dead" (1 Kings 21:7-11,15).

Okay, Ms./Mr. Controller, time to take action. Think of one person or group that you are currently controlling. What do you fear would happen if you treated them with respect by honoring their choices? Is fear and intimidation the only way that you see of holding on to the relationship? Wouldn't you rather earn their genuine love by being caring rather than callous, or are you willing to settle for "fearful submission"? Why not consider going to counseling to get to the root of the deeper issues that may be driving your behavior? For the next week, try not to criticize or rob anyone of his right to choose. Remember that even God gives people the power of choice. Continue this challenge for another two weeks, or as long as it takes to get your controlling attitude under control.

I cannot conclude this section without admonishing you, if you are a controller's victim, to distance yourself from him now to protect your self-esteem and your emotional well-being. He considers your continued acquiescence as acceptance of his behavior. If the controller is your spouse, seek God's guidance for the courage to set guidelines and healthy boundaries—with consequences—for your future interactions.

Day 23

Envy

Exhibiting Envy

■ ■ ■ ■

*Wrath is cruel, and anger is outrageous; but
who is able to stand before envy?*

PROVERBS 27:4 KJV

Have you ever been around someone whose very presence reminded
you of what you should be, could be, or desire to be? Did you find yourself resenting, criticizing, or unfairly judging the person because you did
not have the faith, courage, discipline, or opportunity to pursue your
own goals? If you answered yes to the latter question, envy has you in its
clutches.

Unlike jealousy, which is the fear of being displaced, envy is a feeling
of ill will toward those who possess the thing you want. It is important
to understand this difference. Jealousy says, "I am afraid you are going to
take what I have." Envy, on the other hand, says, "I want what you have
and I resent you for having it!" Rooted in discontentment, envy is one
of the most frequently concealed of all emotions. It can force you into a
cycle of resentment and self-doubt as you start to wonder what it is about
you that keeps you from getting what you desire. Such discontentment
with your situation becomes the breeding ground for insecurity and its
debilitating thoughts: "You don't deserve to have that." "You don't have
the beauty, the brains, the body, the personality, the social standing, the
contacts, or the *whatever* to even dream of such a thing!" Entertaining

such negative thoughts can leave you scorching in the desert of envy and longing for just a drop of the blessings that seem to shower others.

You must come to grips with the reality that there will always be somebody within your various circles of interaction who will enjoy an advantage you desire. Don't fall into the trap of believing that somebody's life is perfect just because she has something you wish you had. Life is much more complex than that. Everybody has at least one aspect of his existence he wishes were different. Trust me, there is somebody who envies you for something you possess. Pray a hedge of protection around your emotions so that envy will not drag you into a pit of insecurity and resentment of others.

Perhaps you are part of a family where, by default, you are the CFO (chief family officer) and therefore the designated problem-solver. That's my role. And, like me, you've probably had the experience of other family members resenting your ability to take charge of a situation. Understand that you are not the problem. The truth of the matter is that they envy your confidence in facing issues head-on and your ability to think clearly, soberly, and objectively in resolving them. They are simply responding out of their own sense of inadequacy. Your mere existence and all that you represent threaten them. Recognize and seek to understand their insecurity and make a reasonable attempt to include them in the decision-making process when possible. Most importantly, maintain a positive, humble attitude. Make a conscious decision to forgive them immediately if they criticize you. This is called life. It is the price you pay for being the competent, confident person you are.

Someone once said, "No man is a complete failure until he begins disliking men who succeed." There are so many aspects of another person's life that you could envy. If you are ready to be truthful with yourself, review the list below and consider if there is a specific individual whom you are envying because of one or more of the advantages or possessions listed. Now, using a scale of one to ten, ten being highest, go a step further and rate your current level of contentment in each of the corresponding areas of potential envy.

Area of Potential Envy	My Contentment Level (1-10)
Financial Security	_____
Professional Achievements	_____
Intelligence/Education	_____
Physical Attractiveness	_____
Youthfulness/Vitality	_____
Confidence/Assertiveness	_____
Place of Residence	_____
Marital Status	_____
Social Standing/Popularity	_____
Successful Children	_____
Being "Privileged" or Favored	_____
Sophistication/Taste	_____
Other: _____	_____

As you named the targeted person of your envy, recall how you have interacted with or discussed her. Have you ever made critical remarks about her? Having completed this exercise, you may have quickly noticed that the higher your personal satisfaction level in a certain area, the less likely you are to experience envy in that area.

The point of this exercise is to begin to make your envy work for you as a source of revelation and motivation. The key question to ask yourself would be: Is it within the realm of possibility for me to obtain the thing that is causing me to envy? Get real about the impossible things such as growing taller, being married to someone else's spouse, and so forth. If it is not possible to obtain the coveted item, then settle it in your heart to accept God's plan for your life. If the coveted thing is a possibility, ask yourself the next question: Am I willing to pay the price to obtain it? The world has a saying: "There ain't no free lunch." You must be willing to pay the price for *everything*. Nothing is free except salvation. So, whether you want to be thin, rich, educated, or whatever, your best bet is to stop envying and get busy. Go toward those who possess what you desire. Find out the secret to their success. Tell them how much you admire them. Indeed you do. Envy is negative admiration! You will find that most people will be flattered and will respond positively to your interest.

Within the next few weeks, seek out someone you have envied. Invite her to lunch or dinner at her favorite restaurant (don't forget to pick up the tab) just to "pick her brain" about an area in which she excels. If she is not immediately available, refuse to perceive her response as personal rejection. Be patient. Persevere.

The Envious Attitude

■ ■ ■ ■

Tendency to downplay someone else's success,
good fortune, qualities, or possessions

Can you handle success? No, not yours; someone else's? Perhaps everyone at some time or another has observed the good fortune of a person and felt discontentment and even resentment. I know I have.

Just a few weeks ago I turned my TV to a popular daytime show and watched Ms. X spout her financial wisdom. I had to admit that she gave sound advice, but when her name came up in our financial Bible study group that night, I confess that I found delight in saying, "I love her advice too. Too bad she's gay."

Some were shocked to learn this; others were already aware of it. What bothered me later was why I had found this to be relevant information to share. Perhaps it was because one of the members was going on and on about how awesome Ms. X was and how much she admired her. Yes, I too admire her; however, what I thought was, *It isn't fair that she's reached such fame and fortune. I deserve that. I'm a straight, Spirit-filled Christian, a submitted wife, and a faithful tither. Yes, I've achieved some level of success, but nothing compared to Ms. X. She's a media darling!* I was ashamed at the carnality of my thinking as I reflected on it later.

When you practice being honest with yourself, the best place to run is to the Scriptures for more revelation and cleansing. That's exactly what I did. The light of God's Word exposed an area that most of us are loath to admit. Envy had reared its head. I thought I had completely slain it eons ago.

What causes an envious attitude? Why do we often criticize someone who has what we desire? And why do we try to tie God's hands from blessing those we feel do not deserve it? What does the Bible say about envy anyway? Is it really a sin or just an unproductive character trait?

Lucifer, whom God had appointed to lead the heavenly host of angels, became envious of God and wanted the worship and adoration God received.

> How you have fallen from heaven,
> morning star, son of the dawn!
> You have been cast down to the earth,
> you who once laid low the nations!
> You said in your heart,
> "I will ascend to the heavens;
> I will raise my throne above the stars of God…
> I will ascend above the tops of the clouds;
> I will make myself like the Most High."
> (Isaiah 14:12-14)

This is our attitude when we envy others. We want the admiration and worship they receive because of the thing they possess. We believe we can be esteemed only if we have what they have.

The last of the Ten Commandments, "You shall not covet" (Exodus 20:17), warns us not to desire anything that someone else possesses. Such an attitude in essence accuses God of being unfair and unaware of what is best for our lives. Therefore, we would be wise to wage an all-out campaign against envy when it shows up in our life. Here's how:

Confess and repent of your impure motives for desiring something other than for the glory of God. "But if you harbor bitter envy and selfish ambition in your hearts, do not boast about it or deny the truth" (James 3:14).

Count your blessings. Envy is rooted in discontentment, and often we are so pained at the good fortune of others that we are blinded to our own advantages. Someone once said, "Envy is the habit of counting someone else's blessings instead of your own."

Understand what your envy is telling you about the decisions, training, and other actions you need to take to fulfill your destiny. Accept that looks or family heritage are beyond your control. Ask God for clarity of His will for you.

Spend time, if possible, with the person you envy to find out more about her and her secrets to success. You may find that she has a host of problems that will curb your envy. A colleague I envied many years ago for her extraordinary beauty told me of her painful childhood abandonment and her battle with insecurity. She confessed that she envied me for my courage to confront thorny issues with intimidating folks. I was shocked.

Rather than making negative comments, speak words of admiration when someone praises a person you are tempted to envy.

Refuse to view another person's success as your failure.

Embracing Individuality

■ ■ ■ ■

One person considers one day more sacred than
another; another considers every day alike. Each of
them should be fully convinced in their own mind.

ROMANS 14:5

I like every single ingredient in vegetable juice: tomatoes, carrots, celery, beets, parsley, lettuce, watercress, and spinach. However, I can hardly stand to drink even the smallest serving of this healthy concoction. On the other hand, if you were to offer me the ingredients in the form of a salad, I'm likely to ask for a second helping. What makes the difference? Individuality! In the vegetable juice, all of the vegetables have been blended together and have lost their distinction. Whereas with the salad, they are all in the same bowl but have retained their uniqueness. So it is with confident people. They are comfortable maintaining their uniqueness while still working in harmony with those who are different.

Some people are just downright scared to embrace their individuality. They would rather live according to the "herd instinct"; all of their actions or decisions are determined by the behavior of the group. The fear of being judged or rejected for being different is too great. Not so with emotionally secure people. They feel no pressure to be a carbon copy of anyone else's style or other aspect of their being.

Women are notorious for resisting individuality. When I have joined in outside activities with other women, I will invariably get a call asking what I'm planning to wear—despite the fact that the official invitation to the event or the nature of the outing itself gave clear indication of what was appropriate. "Are you wearing a dress or pants?" I know that women in general have been socialized to be groupies, but I find few things more refreshing than a woman who is relaxed and comfortable with her own choices.

The apostle Paul modeled individuality. He never tried to emulate the other disciples, who had enjoyed an up-close and personal relationship with Jesus. In fact, when God arrested his heart and called him to preach to the Gentiles, Paul did not solicit any tips or tools of the trade from the more experienced, hands-on disciples who had walked with Jesus on a daily basis. Consider his testimony:

> Then it pleased him to reveal his Son to me so that I would proclaim the Good News about Jesus to the Gentiles. When this happened, I did not rush out to consult with any human being. Nor did I go up to Jerusalem to consult with those who were apostles before I was. Instead, I went away into Arabia, and later I returned to the city of Damascus. Then three years later I went to Jerusalem to get to know Peter, and I stayed with him for fifteen days (Galatians 1:16-18 NLT).

Although Paul could not boast an earthly relationship with Jesus, he did not feel he brought any less to the table—even in light of the fact that he had also persecuted and killed many Christians. He would not allow his negative past to cause him to feel inadequate or unworthy of his divine assignment. Why, he was even confident enough to rebuke Peter for his hypocrisy in eating and fellowshipping with the Gentiles and then ignoring them when the Jews came around (see Galatians 2). Can you imagine this Johnny-come-lately rebuking the great pillar of the church that had so much power that his shadow had actually healed people? Why, you'd have to be the king of confidence to do that.

Emotionally secure people not only have the courage to exercise their uniqueness, but they also support the right of another individual to be different. They do not insist on compliance with their rigid standards that have no basis other than tradition or their personal preferences. Accepting another person's individuality does not mean you approve of their immoral behavior.

Emotionally secure people do not believe that people who are different are inferior—or superior. They do not pass judgment on those who dress differently. Now, I'm not condoning bizarre outfits or wild, God-dishonoring attire; I am promoting a mindset of love and acceptance that transcends mere physical appearance.

Emotionally secure people do not require others to rubber-stamp their ideas or opinions—especially as they relate to nonessential matters. I know two friends who parted ways because they had different opinions about the fairness of a verdict rendered in a high-profile murder case. Whatever happened to respecting the opinion of another? By the way, if you struggle with letting others have their opinion, a key question to ask yourself is, "Will this person's stance on this matter negatively impact my life?" If not, respect it and keep moving. If the matter has eternal consequences—and most matters do not—pray that God will bring him (or maybe you) into the light of the truth.

Emotionally secure people know how to appreciate someone "as is." They realize that if others "zig" where they "zag," a complete picture will be produced rather than an unsolved jigsaw puzzle. Accepting others "as is" is sometimes a bit of a challenge for me because I tend to have quite a few social "shoulds," such as "no smacking," "no white shoes after Labor Day," "no speaking in a loud volume in public," and so forth. I often have to remind myself that even though these may be the rules of etiquette, I have to accept the fact that other people may choose not to abide by them.

Many women have scared off or missed out on good mates by insisting on molding him to their graven image. I would caution any male or female to decide whether he or she can truly accept a potential mate "as is." It is almost a universal paradox that when a person knows he is accepted unconditionally, he then desires to change to show you his appreciation for such acceptance. If you are looking for perfection, stop it. It will always elude you.

Is there an area of your life where you are fearful of being yourself? Why not take a baby step and deliberately exercise a little individuality? Further, the next time someone expresses an opinion contrary to yours, simply nod and say, "I respect your right to differ." Resist the urge to persuade them to agree with you.

Day 24

People-Pleasing

Going Along to Get Along

■ ■ ■ ■

As for me and my household, we will serve the LORD.

Joshua 24:15

"Where in the world is Moses?" That was the question on the mind of the frustrated multitude who had followed him in the Jewish exodus from Egyptian bondage. God had summoned Moses to Mount Sinai to give him instructions and the Ten Commandments for the people. Thing is, God didn't tell Moses or the people how long he would be gone. Moses left Aaron, his people-pleasing brother, in charge.

Forty days passed. The last time anybody had seen Moses, he was disappearing into the fog on his way to the top of the mountain. The restless multitude decided that Moses was never coming back; they approached Aaron.

> "Come on," they said, "make us some gods who can lead us. We don't know what happened to this fellow Moses, who brought us here from the land of Egypt." So Aaron said, "Take the gold rings from the ears of your wives and sons and daughters, and bring them to me." All the people took the gold rings from their ears and brought them to Aaron. Then Aaron took the gold, melted it down, and molded it into the shape of a calf. When the people saw it, they exclaimed, "O Israel, these are the gods who brought you out of Egypt!" (Exodus 32:1-4 NLT).

There. All done. Aaron had pacified them. He had gone along to get along. You will notice in the account of this event that Aaron did not make the slightest protest. His fear of the people caused him to cave in very quickly to their evil demand for a god. When he finished making the calf, the people began a wild celebration by worshipping it as their new god.

But wait! Here comes Moses—and boy, is he angry! He sees the wild party in progress and the worshipping of the golden calf. He is so upset that he threw to the ground and broke into pieces the stone tablets on which God had personally written the Ten Commandments. Without seeking any explanation, he "took the calf the people had made and burned it in the fire; then he ground it to powder, scattered it on the water and made the Israelites drink it" (Exodus 32:20).

Now it was time to confront his brother.

> Finally, he turned to Aaron and demanded, "What did these people do to you to make you bring such terrible sin upon them?" "Don't get so upset, my lord," Aaron replied. "You yourself know how evil these people are. They said to me, 'Make us gods who will lead us. We don't know what happened to this fellow Moses, who brought us here from the land of Egypt.' So I told them, 'Whoever has gold jewelry, take it off.' When they brought it to me, I simply threw it into the fire—and out came this calf!" (Exodus 32:21-24 NLT).

Likely story, Aaron.

Have you ever noticed that insecure people do not "own" or take full responsibility for their actions? Aaron knew he had personally fashioned the golden calf with his tooling equipment, yet he lied and claimed that the calf mysteriously came out of the fire. His fear of displeasing Moses caused him to shift the blame onto the people rather than admitting that he too had sinned by catering to their demand.

No one in a position of authority can afford to be so weak that he compromises his moral standards or personal convictions to avoid being unpopular or losing favor.

Aaron's "please disease" resulted in disastrous consequences. Moses instructed the tribe of the Levites to kill more than 3000 rebellious people that day, including some of their own relatives. Afterward, God sent a plague among the people to punish them further.

When we fast-forward to the time Jesus was on the earth, we notice the same "going along to get along" attitude prevailing among some of the Jewish leaders who really believed that Jesus was indeed the Messiah: "Yet at the same time many even among the leaders believed in him. But because of the Pharisees they would not openly acknowledge their faith for fear they would be put out of the synagogue; for they loved human praise more than praise from God" (John 12:42-43). What a tragedy! These men made a conscious decision to choose social acceptance over eternal life. The thought of alienation from the group was more than they could bear. According to famed psychologist Abraham Maslow, acceptance is one of the basic human needs. However, when we usurp God's authority and decide it is our personal responsibility to get our acceptance needs met, we are prone to making relational decisions that dishonor Him and thwart His purposes in our lives.

It is inherent in the nature of man to want to be in relationship with others. Society punishes lawbreakers by incarcerating them and separating them from their everyday relationships. Even in prison, the most dreaded form of punishment, other than death, is solitary confinement. God Himself declared, "It is not good for the man to be alone" (Genesis 2:18). Clearly, God wants us to be in relationship with others. We run into trouble, however, when we decide we must maintain certain relationships even at the expense of violating God's principles and mandates or His plan for our lives.

When was the last time you went along to get along in order to avoid displeasing someone? What exactly did you fear? What is the worst that would have happened had the thing you feared come to pass?

The Martyr Attitude

■ ■ ■ ■

*Sacrificing or suffering in order to arouse
feelings of pity or guilt in others*

She carries the weight of the world on her shoulders—and she makes sure everyone knows she does.

"I left work early today because I had to take my elderly neighbor to the doctor. He doesn't have any relatives in town."

"I'm so exhausted. I worked 16 hours on that proposal while the rest of the executives sauntered off to happy hour."

"I had to clean the entire house by myself in preparation for our holiday guests. My husband and kids didn't lift a finger to help me."

Sound familiar? Meet the false martyr. She sacrifices out of a false sense of obligation and derives satisfaction and self-esteem from the sympathy and attention it brings her from others. She can be found in every segment of human relationships: marriages, companies, churches, schools, social organizations—you name it.

"But," you may ask, "isn't martyrdom a noble act? What does a *true* martyr look like anyway?"

A true martyr sacrifices his life or personal freedom in order to further a cause or belief for the benefit of many. Famous martyrs include Dr. Martin Luther King Jr., who fought for equal civil rights for the black community, and Dietrich Bonhoeffer, a Lutheran pastor and theologian, killed by the Nazis for his role in openly resisting Adolf Hitler's policies toward the Jews. Unlike the false martyr, these men gave their lives out of a pure passion for a cause. During their lifetime, they did not exalt their personal sacrifice nor wear it as a badge of honor.

A martyr attitude can have a profoundly negative effect on relationships. Others usually find the false martyr exhausting and unpleasant to be around, primarily because false martyrs complain about their service. Further, some martyrs attempt to place a guilt trip on people who do not emulate or appreciate their sacrifices. Most people will resent being manipulated in this manner.

I have had numerous discussions with a false martyr who often accuses me and my husband of being insensitive to the needy simply because we do not broadcast or whine about our benevolence to others as he does. Further, unlike him, we are strongly opposed to enabling irresponsible financial behavior. We refuse to hand out money to people just because they ask for it. He finds every reason to justify his martyr attitude.

What about you? Do you sacrifice for others hoping to gain their favor, love, or loyalty? Do you berate yourself for always putting your needs last? Do you resent certain people for taking you for granted or violating your (usually unspoken) boundaries? Do you feel deep down inside that you do not deserve the benevolence or sacrifices of others? Do you find it difficult to ask for help for fear that you will become obligated to someone? If you are ready to free yourself from this mindset, try these strategies for the next 30 days:

Serve sincerely. "Don't just pretend to love others. Really love them" (Romans 12:9 NLT). Be honest about your real objective for sacrificing for others. Only God knows your true motive, and He has given you the Bible to help you to discern it. "For the word of God is alive and active. Sharper than any double-edged sword, it…judges the thoughts and attitudes of the heart" (Hebrews 4:12). I suggest reading a chapter from Proverbs each morning for wisdom, guidance, and purification of your motives.

Serve silently. Stop mentioning or complaining about the sacrifices you're making. This habit may be entrenched, so you'll have to catch yourself before you indulge. This is an easy attitude to fall into if you tend to be the go-to person in most of your circles of interaction. Just today, I caught myself complaining about three different sacrifices that I had decided to make in the midst of my tight writing schedule. I stopped and reminded myself that God gives us aptitudes, skills, and resources to be used for His glory. "From everyone who has been given much, much will be demanded; and from the one who has been entrusted with much, much more will be asked" (Luke 12:48). Refuse to complain about what God asks you to do— when you know for sure He is asking.

Serve selectively. Pray before you make a personal sacrifice. Be sure that it is a "God idea" and not just a "good idea" borne out of your need to be needed. If you think you cannot make the sacrifice out of a sincere and obedient heart, or you do not feel the peace of God to proceed, pray for the courage to say no.

Saying No

■ ■ ■ ■

I have brought you glory on earth by
finishing the work you gave me to do.

JOHN 17:4

Jesus compassionately performed many miracles; however, there were times when He knew He had to move on to the next place in order to spread the gospel. Notwithstanding, sick people were still coming to Him, and His disciples were anxious for Him to heal them. On one occasion, His disciples sought Him while He was alone praying. "When they found Him, they exclaimed, 'Everyone is looking for you!' Jesus replied, 'Let us go somewhere else—to the nearby villages—so I can preach there also. That is why I have come'" (Mark 1:37-38). Did Jesus really say no to performing additional miracles? Yes. He knew exactly what His priorities were and He stayed focused. Therefore, He was able to report to His heavenly Father at the end of life, "I have brought you glory on earth by finishing the work you gave me to do" (John 17:4). Nothing more. Nothing less.

Do you find it hard to say no even when you are being distracted from your purpose and goals? For most people, saying yes when they really wish to say no raises their stress level by several degrees. Obviously, when they do so, they are trying to avoid some potentially negative consequences, such as rejection, loss of favor, and so forth. If you find yourself faced with such a dilemma, it is a good exercise to stop for a moment and mentally play out the entire scenario of what you think will happen when you say no. The only way to overcome your fear or insecurity in this area is to start to take small risks until you are finally comfortable delivering a firm no. It eats away at your sense of self-worth to feel that you have relinquished your power of choice over to someone else. Whenever I have done this in the past, I felt angry with myself and deep resentment toward the person I could not bring myself to disappoint. I have been healed from the tendency for many years and enjoy the freedom of living with my own choices. Let's see if you can get into practice with a couple of scenarios.

Situation A: Your friend Jack has just asked you to lend him $500 until he gets on his feet. You know that Jack is financially irresponsible, and you really and truly do not want to make the loan. Plus, granting his request would cut you short on the emergency cash reserve you are building. Let's say that you tell him, "Jack, I can't do that." How do you think he will respond? How will his response affect the quality of your life thereafter? Will he pout for a while, tell all your other friends that you are stingy, or attempt to tarnish your image in some way? Do you have the emotional strength to handle any of these scenarios? Is your relationship with him so crucial to your well-being that you feel it is better to grant the loan than to bear such consequences?

Situation B: Suppose that Suzie is relocating to Beth's city and asks Beth to let her move into her apartment until she can find her own place. She knows that Beth has a spare bedroom. Beth is well aware that Suzie is quite messy. Beth tends to be a neat freak. In fact, the sight of untidiness really impacts Beth's sense of peace. Beth and Suzie have been friends for 20 years and are very close. Suzie has always been there for Beth through all Beth's ups and downs. Beth has just remodeled her place to suit her lifestyle and needs. Her extra bedroom now doubles as her office, except when she has an occasional weekend guest.

Should Beth tell Suzie no because she doesn't want to be inconvenienced? Sometimes no is not the right or godly answer for a situation. While it is good and emotionally healthy to learn to establish boundaries, we must guard against becoming selfish and unwilling to sacrifice for others. Sometimes a yes with very clear boundaries will go a long way in preserving your peace and your relationships. For example, Beth and Suzie would do well to agree upon how long Suzie will stay. Further, it is imperative that Beth communicate her quirks and druthers from how she likes the refrigerator organized to her desired curfew on a ringing telephone. I have found that a mere discussion is often not enough. I'm a firm believer in writing preferences down and reviewing them with the related party. This can be done in a lighthearted manner so that it doesn't seem so impersonal. For instance, Beth could say, "Suzie, you never know a person until you live with them, so I want to share with you some of my little quirks and eccentricities—and I'd like you to share yours as well." In addition to a commitment to the friendship, getting Suzie's preferences on the table shows consideration and fairness on Beth's part and keeps them both from having to walk on eggshells with each other.

I am amazed at the number of people who find it almost impossible to have a conversation like the one above. Trust me, it gets easier and easier the more you do it. I'd dare say that all my friends and guests know my preferences, pet peeves, and quirks. In fact, in my guest room I have a short list of preferred behavior for all who visit overnight or for an extended period of time. Some have asked me for a copy for their own use. It is not at all mean-spirited; it is merely designed to make their stay comfortable and without aggravation to us or them.

Parents are another group that would experience a lot less stress if they would just exercise some strength and stick to their guns. I have watched children test the limits just like a swimmer testing the water temperature with her feet. Children want boundaries. They need them. I have lots of nieces and nephews, and it's amazing to see the respect with which some of them respond to me versus their anything-goes parents. Spanking is not always the answer, but there should be some immediate and undesirable consequences for bad behavior.

Finally, do not be subtly manipulated into saying yes due to obvious circumstances. Some people may hint but never ask directly. If you know that your saying yes to an indirect request or supplying a need is going to be an enabling act, then look straight ahead and say, "I'll believe God with you that He will work things out." For example, my friend whom I'll call "Annie" called and asked for my prayers for her friend Sally, who has struggled financially for what seems like forever. As I queried her more about Sally's situation, it became clear to me that Annie and others have been part of the problem by always responding personally to her requests for prayer for her various financial needs. Annie did not want to face the fact that she was being manipulated. I told Annie that rather than praying for Sally, I was going to pray that God would take the scales from her own eyes so that she could see the situation for what it was and get the courage to confront and minister to Sally in a life-changing way.

"No" is a complete sentence, and it will help you lower your stress and stay sane when applied with wisdom.

Day 25

Perfectionism

The Perfect Performance

■ ■ ■ ■

*But by the grace of God I am what I am, and his grace to
me was not without effect. No, I worked harder than all of
them—yet not I, but the grace of God that was with me.*

1 CORINTHIANS 15:10

Do you feel that what you accomplish is never really good enough?
Are you slow to make a decision or turn in a project because you must
make sure it is just right? If you answered yes to either of these questions,
are you ready to leave the prison of perfectionism?

Perfectionism is a mindset of self-defeating thoughts and behaviors
aimed at reaching unrealistic goals. Famed psychologist Dr. David Viscott
explained it this way:

> A controlling adult's wish to be perfect stems from the child-
> hood wish to be blameless. Since real growth means embrac-
> ing your faults and examining your weaknesses, controlling
> people run the greatest risk of becoming rigid and failing
> because of their insistence on being right. They need to feel
> they are beyond criticism so that no one will have a good rea-
> son for withholding what they need or rejecting them. They
> believe they need to be perfect just to be safe, so admitting even
> small imperfections makes them uneasy and self-doubting. If
> they can be imperfect in one way, they reason, they could

be imperfect in others. Since being imperfect is a fact of life, acknowledging themselves honestly is a continual threat to their self-esteem. Even slight criticisms compel them to refute others' logic and testimony.*

There are those who, rather than seeking to perfect their relationship with God, choose instead to gain man's accolades through perfect performance. I have dealt with my own performance perfectionism with some success. For example, when I worked in the corporate world, I often demanded perfection from my staff. I now know my real fear was that any mistakes they made would cause others to think I was personally incompetent. My department was high profile because it served the entire organization. It seemed that the staff was bent on sabotaging my image— or that's how I perceived it since the buck stopped with me. They knew I did not tolerate poor performance; therefore, they felt that each mistake brought them closer to being fired.

After a series of staff mistakes, I was at my wit's end. I had documented procedures, encouraged questions, maintained an open-door policy, and had done all that I knew to ensure an efficient operation. I earnestly prayed for a breakthrough. God gave me a new mindset and a new strategy for the situation. I called a staff meeting and set everyone free from perfection prison. I asked them to do their very best and to develop systems or procedures to avoid repeating the same mistakes in the future. I even confessed several mistakes I had made on the job that I'd never shared with them. A marvelous thing happened. Their anxiety levels dropped and morale soared. The finger-pointing virtually stopped because team solutions became more important than placing blame. In our staff meetings, we even started to find humor in some of the errors— which, by the way, decreased significantly. It was never my intention for my pursuit of excellence to turn into an anxiety-producing perfectionism that negatively affected the quality of people's lives.

Performance perfectionists must learn to enjoy the *process* of achieving their goals without obsessing over the end result. They must become flexible and mature enough to solicit and pay attention to honest feedback.

---

*   David Viscott, *Emotionally Free* (Chicago, IL: Contemporary Books, 1992), 54.

Most importantly, perfectionists must submit all of their plans to God and believe He will work things out for good as they follow His leading.

Perfectionism can rob you of the peace, productivity, and personal satisfaction you can experience once you accept the weaknesses, imperfections, and shortcomings inherent in being human. Remember, Noah, an amateur guided by God, built the ark while professionals, using the best of man's wisdom, built the *Titanic*. The ark fulfilled its purpose; the *Titanic* sank.

Dying to Be Beautiful

■ ■ ■ ■

Charm is deceptive, and beauty is fleeting; but a
woman who fears the LORD is to be praised.

PROVERBS 31:30

Obesity is the number one health concern in the United States. However, it is not generally obese people who obsess over their physical appearance. Rather, it is primarily those—especially women—who are already within an acceptable weight range that strive to achieve physical perfection. I live in Southern California where it seems that physical beauty is worshipped more than God. Of course, the presence of the television and film industry with its skilled makeup and makeover artists has established a beauty standard that only a few can achieve. Hollywood's influence has permeated the entire country and even the world. It is no wonder insecurity reigns among the masses.

Some people become insecure even about their best features. For example, suppose people often tell a woman that she has beautiful hair, teeth, or skin. Before long, she may start obsessing over ways to make sure that the complimented feature is always perfect. Some women have actually ruined something that was naturally beautiful by trying to perfect it.

The big question here is how far should God's children go to maximize their attractiveness? What does the Bible say about altering the unique deck of physical cards God has dealt? He dictated our unchangeable physical features before we even entered this world. The psalmist declared, "You made all the delicate, inner parts of my body and knit me together in my mother's womb" (Psalm 139:13 NLT). According to the prophet Isaiah, each aspect of our body was designed to fulfill His divine purpose. "And now the LORD speaks—the one who formed me in my mother's womb to be his servant" (Isaiah 49:5 NLT).

God deliberately shaped each of us for His service. How then can we complain that we are too short, too tall, too dark, too fair, or too anything that is unchangeable? The word "too" implies that something is beyond what is desirable or more than what should be. Such a declaration about God's creation is a rejection of His judgment. How can something God formed be *too* anything? What we are really saying is, "This feature does not conform to society's prescribed standard of beauty." Thus, we allow our nonconforming attributes to cause us to become insecure and rob us of our confidence. We then feel that our only solution is to change the undesirable feature. What a slap in God's face. Listen to what He has to say about our rejection of His judgment:

> What sorrow awaits those who argue with their Creator.
> Does a clay pot argue with its maker?
> Does the clay dispute with the one who shapes it, saying,
> "Stop, you're doing it wrong!"
> Does the pot exclaim,
> "How clumsy can you be?"
> How terrible it would be if a newborn baby said to its father,
> "Why was I born?"
> or if it said to its mother,
> "Why did you make me this way?"
> This is what the Lord says—
> the Holy One of Israel and your Creator:
> "Do you question what I do for my children?
> Do you give me orders about the work of my hands?"
>   (Isaiah 45:9-11 NLT).

Because we cannot perfect what God has already perfected for His purpose, our objective should be to accept the work of His hands. How do we do this? Does accepting our features mean we have to like them? You will strengthen your emotional security when you make peace with every aspect of yourself. By God's grace and divine enablement, you must truly accept—not merely resign yourself to—His sovereign design. When you do so, you stop comparing yourself to others and judging yourself inferior or superior. Self-consciousness and fretting with the outward appearance disappear. You have now cleared the path for your real, inner beauty to shine through.

Of course, the big question among Christian women is whether to undergo corrective surgery. If a physical attribute *detracts* from your ability to communicate or to be effective, and God gives you the means and the go-ahead to correct it, then by all means proceed.

In my early twenties I dated a young man who had a front tooth that was significantly larger than its mate. He was a brilliant up-and-coming junior executive with great oratory skills. Unfortunately, I could not help but focus on that tooth the entire time he was speaking. I finally mustered the courage to recommend a good dentist, who subsequently capped and brought alignment to his front teeth. His smile and his confidence improved significantly. The last I heard of him, he was still climbing the corporate ladder.

What is the condition of your smile? Investing in the best smile you can afford is money well spent. Your smile can be your most effective calling card and an instant reflection of the love of God in your heart.

If filling a gap between your teeth, having a prominent mole removed, incorporating a wave into thinning hair, or correcting any other distracting feature will enhance your effectiveness, it will be money put to good use and do wonders for your self-esteem. Don't wait for someone else to point this out to you. Just take an honest look in the mirror. Or ask an honest friend who really loves you and has the courage to tell you the truth. Remember that the primary purpose of any physical correction should be to eliminate or minimize distractions for your message rather than trying to perfect God's design. Even my advice herein is not a divine mandate. "In all your ways submit to him, and he will make your paths straight" (Proverbs 3:6).

Abandoning physical perfection is not about liking yourself but about trusting God enough to accept and rejoice in His physical design. It is time to experience body peace. You are designed for your destiny, tailored for your tasks, and perfect for your purpose. Know that your vulnerabilities and weaknesses often make you more relatable and endearing to others.

Identify specific perfectionist behaviors in various areas of your life (spiritual, performance, physical) and commit to overcoming at least one thing now.

Admitting Mistakes and Shortcomings

■ ■ ■ ■

Therefore confess your sins to each other and pray for each other so that you may be healed.

JAMES 5:16

"I'm sorry I was wrong." "My mistake!" "I don't know." These are words that some people find hard to say. Just the other day, I was talking to a man who blamed his former girlfriend for having his child out of wedlock and then not forcing him to have a relationship with his son for the past 25 years. "She should have put more pressure on me," he said. "I would have acknowledged him and made him a part of my life. But now look how much time has passed. Besides, she did not give him my last name." I asked him, "Is that an excuse to avoid having a relationship with him now?" It seems that everywhere you turn somebody is making an excuse for his poor choices, performance, or behavior, or failing to admit a weakness or shortcoming.

Staying blameless is a hard and stressful position to maintain. Everybody makes a mistake, misjudges an issue, or otherwise messes up something at some point. It's called being human. Oddly enough, mistakes are one of the major ways we learn. However, because of our fear of being judged negatively or losing face, we often try to cover up our mistakes—which opens the door wide for stress. On the other hand, admitting a mistake is a surefire stress-buster. It is a relief to yourself and an inspiration to others when you show the courage and the confidence to acknowledge your mistakes without defining yourself by them.

The only real tragedy about mistakes is if you don't learn anything from them. Refusing to admit a mistake closes the door for growth. Hear the words of the Lord when He admonished the Israelites to learn from their mistakes. "When people fall down, do they not get up? When someone turns away, do they not return?'" (Jeremiah 8:4).

Like Adam in the Garden of Eden, who tried to blame Eve when he ate the forbidden fruit, many people make every effort to avoid accepting personal responsibility. Circumstances and other people may have had an influence on our decisions; however, in the final analysis we are responsible for what we do. When we make a mistake, our action was our choice. Aaron made the golden calf in the wilderness because the people were getting restless about Moses's absence. However, upon his return, Moses indicted him—not the people.

The best strategy for dealing with your mistakes is to accept full responsibility, determine how not to repeat them, and move on. While this sounds simple, it is not easy. You may worry that your critics will judge you harshly, but I assure you that if you continue this pattern of dealing with mistakes, it will become easier and easier and will inspire others to emulate your behavior. What does it buy you to struggle to stay on that Blameless Pedestal? Absolutely nothing but stress. When I have found myself being unjustifiably defensive, I feel the adrenaline rush to provide the fight-or-flight energy I need to fight for my stance and to run from taking personal responsibility. On the other hand, I experience the peace of God when I admit a mistake. It relaxes me and frees my mind to focus on what to do next in dealing with the problem.

In addition to creating stress, there is another downside to an attempt to be blameless. When you deny your shortcomings and mistakes, people are likely to label you as arrogant and proud. The irony is that others connect with you better and will declare you humble when you admit your weaknesses. Humility is one of the traits that people admire most in others; pride is detested—even by other proud folks.

One of the best biblical examples of admitting a mistake is found in the account of David being unjustly pursued by King Saul. David became a fugitive and in the process unknowingly jeopardized the lives of certain priests when he asked for their help. Ahimelech the priest gave him food and a sword and inquired of God on his behalf. Doeg, King Saul's chief herdsman, witnessed the whole thing and squealed on the priest. Saul confronted Ahimelech, accused him of conspiring with David, and ordered Doeg to kill him and 85 other priests and their entire families. "Only Abiathar, one of the sons of Ahimelech, escaped and fled to David. When he told David that Saul had killed the priests of the LORD,

David exclaimed, 'I knew it! When I saw Doeg the Edomite there that day, I knew he was sure to tell Saul. Now I have caused the death of all your father's family'" (1 Samuel 22:20-22 NLT). What an admission! No excuses. Just an acknowledgment that he had made a mistake in seeking their help. His next statement shows his commitment to not repeating the mistake with the remaining survivor: "Stay here with me, and don't be afraid. I will protect you with my own life, for the same person wants to kill us both" (1 Samuel 22:23 NLT).

Humans make mistakes. They have blind spots. God is present to support our every weakness. Peace comes when we start confessing our faults to one another.

Day 26

The Values-Driven Life

Letting Your Values Do the Driving

■ ■ ■ ■

*As I looked at everything I had worked so hard to
accomplish, it was all so meaningless—like chasing the
wind. There was nothing really worthwhile anywhere.*

ECCLESIASTES 2:11 NLT

What are your guiding principles? What drives your behavior? Is it the
quest for the finer things of life? Or maybe you are in pursuit of social status or you simply desire to achieve perfection in your endeavors. Whatever
the motivation, is it worth the stress it causes you? Let's see how our Savior
dealt with one woman's self-imposed stress.

One day Jesus and His disciples stopped for a visit at the home of
Martha and Mary. Martha, being the consummate hostess, fretted about
trying to get everything just right for her guests. Mary, however, had a
different agenda. She chose to sit and listen to Jesus talk. Martha wasn't
having it. She needed Mary to give her a hand, so she appealed to Jesus.

> She came to Jesus and said, "Lord, doesn't it seem unfair to you
> that my sister just sits here while I do all the work? Tell her to
> come and help me." But the Lord said to her, "My dear Mar-
> tha, you are so upset over all these details! There is only one
> thing worth being concerned about. Mary has discovered it,
> and it will not be taken away from her" (Luke 10:40-42 NLT).

Unfortunately for Martha, Jesus backed Mary. Mary's behavior said, "I value the opportunity to sit at the feet of Jesus and to feast on His words; therefore, that's where I'm going to invest my time and energy." This is not a story about prayer but about bringing our values and our behavior into alignment. Martha was not a bad person; she simply had misplaced values.

Values serve as our internal compass. Even corporations have developed "values-driven" principles that dictate their actions. Many post them in their hallways and common areas for all employees to see and embrace. It also keeps the corporation accountable. One very popular Christian organization has as one of its core values the importance of the family. Therefore, it is not their policy to have employees working overtime except when absolutely necessary. Their personnel policies are also family friendly.

Because our values are our internal navigation system, when we choose a course of action that is inconsistent with these values, stress is often the result. Let's take a look at a few scripturally based values that can help to minimize the stress in our lives.

God's Sovereignty. "You saw me before I was born. Every day of my life was recorded in your book. Every moment was laid out before a single day had passed" (Psalm 139:16 NLT). We can rest in the knowledge that God has the last word on everything that concerns us. When all is said and done, we have an ordained destiny. While God does not show us the parade of our lives from start to finish, we know that He is our drum major and we must simply march to His beat.

For example, from a professional perspective, He orchestrates the timing of our promotions, our exposure to influential people, and all other aspects of our careers. It is an insult to His omnipotence when we engage in back-stabbing, dirty politics, strategic maneuverings, and other stress-inducing efforts designed to advance our ball down the court. This does not mean that we shouldn't do a great job or express our desires or preferences to those who can grant them. Further, we should readily walk into a door that He opens and interact with key people He brings into our paths. It all has to do with where we put our faith—in self-efforts or in God's sovereignty.

Integrity. "Honesty guides good people" (Proverbs 11:3). If we walk in integrity, we will experience the peace of knowing that we have done right in the sight of God. Integrity is not just being honest or telling the truth, but also making what you say be the truth. You make your word your bond. When others know they can depend on you to keep your word, it eliminates their stress as well. I know someone who rarely keeps his word. When he promises me something, I hardly dare to hope. In Psalm 15:4, David says that one of the traits of those who will abide in God's eternal presence is that they "keep their promises even when it hurts" (NLT).

Humility. Humility is not a sense of unworthiness, but rather an acceptance of our God-given strengths and our God-allowed weaknesses. We rest in the knowledge of both. Our strengths should not make us proud. Our weaknesses should not make us anxious, for as God declared to the apostle Paul, "My grace is sufficient for you, for my power is made perfect in weakness" (2 Corinthians 12:9).

Equality. No person is better or more important than another. Some have simply had more access to what the world offers, achieved more education, or been called to higher levels of authority and responsibility. No one is inherently better. No one. The ground is level at the foot of the cross. No matter what our station is in life, we are to treat everyone with the same respect.

Generosity. "Give, and it will be given to you. A good measure, pressed down, shaken together and running over, will be poured into your lap. For with the measure you use, it will be measured to you" (Luke 6:38). We are never more like God than when we give, and we can never beat Him at giving. We have no need to be anxious about not having enough if we extend generosity to others.

The list above is not exhaustive of all Christian values. Your list may include others. The important thing is that you allow your core values to become the internal force that drives your actions. To behave in any fashion inconsistent with these values will rob you of your peace.

Doing the Right Thing

■ ■ ■ ■

"There is no peace for the wicked," says the LORD.

Isaiah 48:22 NLT

Sin stresses the body and robs us of our peace. It is interesting to note how a person's nervous system responds to a polygraph exam, commonly referred to as a "lie detector test." The fact is that the test cannot determine if someone is lying. It simply measures how a person's response to certain questions impacts his nervous system. God designed our system to glorify Him by conducting our lives in a holy and righteous manner. When we sin, the stress it causes negatively impacts our entire body. Even if you have never taken a polygraph exam, you can agree that when you have lied you probably experienced an increase in your heart rate.

Whenever we choose a course of action inconsistent with what we believe to be the right thing to do, stress will usually be the result. For example, because of a need for financial survival, a person may accept a job or assignment that requires him to do something contrary to his spiritual convictions, such as serving liquor or working on Sundays. For him, the thought of going to work stresses him. Many people have faced the dilemma of compromising their values in order to get a promotion or to achieve other advantages. To them it seemed to be their only option. Scripture reminds us that "there is a way that appears to be right, but in the end it leads to death" (Proverbs 16:25).

Death is the ultimate separation. Compromise will stress you and separate you from the peace that comes with doing right. This is where a strong spiritual foundation is crucial. It takes faith and courage to let our convictions dictate our behavior and our choices. When Daniel, the Jewish captive who had risen to prominence in Babylon, prayed to God in violation of the king's decree, he faced the risk and ultimately the reality of being thrown into a den of lions. He placed a high premium on prayer and was willing to pay the price to maintain it as an integral part of his life. God honored his faith and shut the mouths of the lions. The king, realizing that he had been duped into signing the decree, ordered Daniel's enemies to be destroyed. Daniel continued to enjoy a long and distinguished career (Daniel 6).

You can eliminate a lot of your stress on the job by giving God the reins of your career. Yes, let management know of your desire to advance within the company, but understand that God is ultimately responsible for your progression. "No one...can exalt themselves. It is God who judges: He brings one down, he exalts another" (Psalm 75:6-7). Rest on this truth and focus on being excellent and on being a team player. Obey company policies, don't cheat in any manner, and watch God do His thing.

Don't think you can do right in your own strength. Sometimes the temptation to retaliate, to lie, or to advance your ball down the court will be too much to resist if you don't stay God-conscious. Don't stress out or give up all hope if you fall. Learn a lesson, repent, and get back on the wagon. Seek God daily to give you the grace to be like Jesus. There is a line in an old hymn that says, "I need Thee every hour." Indeed we do.

The Downside of Dishonesty

■ ■ ■ ■

The integrity of the upright guides them: but the
unfaithful are destroyed by their duplicity.

PROVERBS 11:3

We were down to the wire on getting bank financing for our real estate purchase. We were perplexed. We had excellent credit and a big down payment, but the banks refused to extend us a loan. After seeking the Lord one night, the Holy Spirit revealed to me that the mortgage broker had embellished our personal financial information by overstating certain rental income and other revenues. The Lord sternly warned me that the application must reflect the truth. I was reluctant to say anything to Darnell because I knew that he would insist that the application be corrected immediately. He has an extremely "black and white" mindset when it comes to matters of integrity. He asserts that he simply doesn't deal in gray areas. I, on the other hand, silently rationalized that perhaps this was going to be a situation in which God was doing a "Rahab" deal. Rahab was the harlot who lied about the whereabouts of the Jewish spies so that the Jericho soldiers would not catch them (Joshua 2). The Jews had gone to check out that city which they would ultimately conquer. With the Rahab precedent in mind, I figured God was thinking of using an unholy person (the mortgage broker) to bring deliverance or a blessing to the righteous (that would be us). Okay, so it was a stretch—but I was getting desperate for the deal to close.

Despite my rationalization, the Holy Spirit's conviction prevailed. I called the broker, pointed out the inconsistencies, and insisted that only the truth be reflected in the application. As a result, a bank approved the financing within days. I realized that once we have been exposed to God's

Word, we cannot sin and maintain peace of mind; "Righteousness and peace kiss each other" (Psalm 85:10).

Many times, in the midst of adverse financial circumstances, we often doubt whether God is going to come through for us. We may get anxious and conclude that we had better fix the situation the best way we know how. At other times, the issue may not be one of adverse circumstances, but just the battle against plain old unadulterated greed. Whatever the motivation, in times like these, many will often make the unwise decision to resort to dishonest measures. When we do so, we are in effect saying to God, "I need or desire more resources than I currently have, but I don't believe that you will provide them. Therefore, I'll make my own way through ungodly means." This pitfall is a slap in God's face. It robs Him of the opportunity to be glorified.

We are commanded to walk in integrity. Integrity is simply the act of *integrating* what we say we believe and what we actually do; telling the whole truth and not part of it for personal gain. Yes, even professing Christians can have an integrity problem. When we fail in this area, the integrity disconnection screams out to others. Many unsaved folks are turned off to Christianity by such hypocrisy.

Further, dishonesty can severely impact our ability to exercise faith. As the Scripture says, "Dear friends, if our hearts do not condemn us, we have confidence before God and receive from him anything we ask, because we keep his commandments and do what pleases him" (1 John 3:21-22). It can be hard to believe that God is going to do something special for you if you have been dishonest in your dealings. Guilt and condemnation will be constant reminders to you that you don't deserve the grace of God. And when do we ever deserve it?

Many times, doing the right thing has a relational cost. Just because you have decided to walk in integrity doesn't mean that everyone will continue to embrace you. I have lost relationships with Christians and non-Christians because I have refused to go along with their ungodly proposals. My prayer to God is that He won't let me rest with any dishonesty. Just the other day, a vendor treated me unfairly by withholding a "re-stocking" fee from my merchandise refund. I had just purchased the unopened, non-customized merchandise the day before. I was so frustrated that I wanted to punish him in some way. When he turned his back,

Satan whispered, "Just take his stapler with you." Now, did I need a cheap stapler? No! Satan was just trying to get me to compromise my integrity by retaliating. That's why I have asked God to trouble my conscious so that I can't sleep, function, or go forward in any endeavor where I am not operating in complete integrity.

Dishonest behavior will not only destroy your peace, it will open the back door for your blessings to escape—even if you are a tither. Sure, God has promised to open the windows of heaven and to pour out blessings to the tither, but we must make sure we keep the back door of dishonesty slammed shut at all cost. Otherwise, our blessings will end up in pockets with holes in them, leaving us to wonder what happened.

Day 27

The Pursuit of Peace

Experiencing Peace

■ ■ ■ ■

*Peace I leave with you; my peace I give you. I do
not give to you as the world gives. Do not let your
hearts be troubled and do not be afraid.*

JOHN 14:27

Peace, the absence of anxiety, is the most valuable commodity in the world. It eludes many as they search for it through fame, success, promotion, power, attention, money, or possessions. All the wrong places. Unfortunately, nothing external will ever produce peace of mind. The uncertainties of modern living can keep us in a state of anxiety about real and imagined fears. Using the word *peace* as an acronym, let's take a brief look at some of the basic requirements for inner tranquility.

P—Prioritize every aspect of your life according to God's Word. You must put first things first, especially in the areas of relationships and finances, if you want to experience peace. God and family—in that order—must occupy their rightful places in your heart *and* schedule. The media bombards us weekly with the news of the latest breakup between couples who have achieved fame and fortune. When couples split, it is evident that one or both parties are out of step with God's mandates for successful relationships. But, when both march to the beat of the same drummer, they will walk in cadence with each other.

Obeying God's financial priorities will eliminate anxiety and insecurity about your future ability to maintain the wealth you have gained as a result of your success. It is when you have heaped your wealth on yourself, bought trappings to bolster your worth, and closed your ears to the needy that you experience emotional unrest.

E—Expect less from people and more from God. Have you ever had high expectations of someone who failed you or dashed your hopes? Human beings are prone to disappointing us—not deliberately, but simply because they are mere humans, made from the dust of the earth. We must extend to them the grace that our Father extends to us when we disappoint Him.

On her dying bed, my mentor, the late Dr. Juanita Smith, explained how she had dealt with people who had disappointed or hurt her. She said, "We all hurt people. Many times people don't know they have hurt us. That's why we have to release everybody; we have to forgive." She knew God had a divine purpose in allowing her to suffer failed expectations; she also knew He had given her grace to endure them.

If you want to cultivate peace in your life, start redirecting your expectations toward God. The psalmist cautioned himself, "My soul, wait silently for God alone, for my expectation is from him" (Psalm 62:5 NKJV). Whatever anyone does toward you, always be mindful that God could have stopped them at any point along the way, but He chose not to. Obviously, He deemed your spiritual growth and maturity a greater necessity.

A—Acknowledge God in all your decisions. Because most of us tend to act like "human doings" rather than "human beings," we sometimes fail to determine whether we are in God's will or not. Rather, we often pursue the first great-sounding idea that pops in our minds. Nothing is more frustrating than to expend tremendous effort on an endeavor, only to have God come along and say, "No."

Jehoshaphat, one of the good kings of Judah, learned this lesson when he entered into a partnership with the wicked king of Israel to construct a fleet of trading ships. God sent him a devastating message, "'Because you have made an alliance with Ahaziah, the LORD will destroy what you have made.' The ships were wrecked and were not able to set sail to trade" (2 Chronicles 20:37). All the capital expenditures, the labor cost, and the mental energy that went into the undertaking were all for nothing.

Sometimes in such situations, God will extend grace and bail us out; other times He sits back and allows us to learn the lesson that every *good* idea is not a *God* idea.

C—Cultivate an attitude of contentment. Emotionally secure people have *learned* how to practice peace. The apostle Paul explained, "I have learned to be content whatever the circumstances. I know what it is to be in need, and I know what it is to have plenty. I have learned the secret of being content in any and every situation, whether well fed or hungry, whether living in plenty or in want" (Philippians 4:11-12).

Some people have engaged in extreme thinking and assumed that God wants them to have very little. As such, they extol the virtues of poverty and the denial of material things as the key to peace and contentment. Bible teacher Chip Ingram once said, "Prosperity does not have the power to give us contentment, nor poverty the power to take it away."

E—Eliminate all unrighteousness. Righteousness is simply being in right standing with God. Walking uprightly before Him is foundational to inner peace. We have to make the connection and understand that "righteousness and peace kiss each other" (Psalm 85:10). There is an intimate relationship between doing right and experiencing peace. Sin disconnects us from our power source, the one and only God who enables us to be adequate and sufficient for every task. High moral living puts you under the umbrella of His protection and shields you from the uncertainty that haunts those who are disobedient.

There is a calm assurance, a noticeable sense of peace that emanates from those whose trust in the Lord. They do not have a scarcity mentality that causes them to hesitate to help others; they joyously cooperate. They know their destiny is sealed. Secure people walk in peace because they have learned to put their negative *thoughts* to rest even though their negative *circumstances* may prevail. They are free of emotional turbulence. They know that to walk in confidence, they must cast down every thought that is inconsistent with what they know about God.

In light of the truth that all of the days ordained for us were written in God's book before one of them came to be (Psalms 139:16), name one thing that you have decided to stop fretting about. How will your behavior or conversation change as a result of this decision?

The Contentious Attitude

■ ■ ■ ■

*Quarrelsome, frequently engaging in
arguments and disputes*

"No matter what I say, she always has a 'but' even when we discuss issues neither of us really cares about," George said. "I wonder why she loves arguing so much!"

His exasperation was evident. I knew his wife and silently agreed that she was one contentious woman. A biblical proverb came to mind as I listened to his plight. "It is better to live on a corner of the roof than share a house with a quarrelsome wife" (Proverbs 25:24).

Married women, listen up. If your husband has retreated to the "corner of the housetop" emotionally and has virtually stopped communicating, consider whether your attitude drove him there. How easy are you to talk to? Do you really listen to your husband with the intent to understand, or do you make snap judgments about his behavior? Your attitude establishes the fragrance of your home; you choose whether it will be pleasant or whether it stinks.

It has been my joy for over 30 years to create an atmosphere of peace, lightheartedness, acceptance of differences, and honest and direct communication in our home. I make every effort to inspire my husband by affirming and supporting him and his goals. Nagging has not been necessary.

> A quarrelsome wife is like the dripping
> of a leaky roof in a rainstorm.
> (Proverbs 27:15)

Yes, husbands can be contentious too; however, such an attitude is more common among women. And no, I'm not absolving husbands of their responsibility as the spiritual leader of the home to love, protect, and provide for their family. Few things will cause a woman to become more contentious than when he drops the ball in these areas.

Contentiousness is annoying to everybody—except fellow quarrelers. I heard about an amusing bumper sticker that read: "People who think they know it all are especially annoying to those of us who do."

Of course, nagging wives are not the only ones prone to displaying a contentious attitude. It is also prevalent among older people who, fearing uselessness, struggle to prove they still have some level of superior knowledge. Also guilty are the many people of various religious persuasions who contend for their faith, but have not learned to do it in a non-contentious way—even within their own religious group. I've heard stories of people almost coming to blows in a Sunday school class. They have yet to learn that quarreling does not invite change.

What about you? Do you always have to have the last word in a discussion? Do you feel compelled to argue every issue? God's stance on contentiousness is clear: "Don't have anything to do with foolish and stupid arguments, because you know they produce quarrels. And the Lord's servant must not be quarrelsome but must be kind to everyone, able to teach, not resentful" (2 Timothy 2:23-24). This passage shows four key strategies for overcoming a contentious attitude.

"Must not be quarrelsome." You really can cut off contention at the pass by simply refusing to engage in a going-nowhere-positive conversation. "Starting a quarrel is like breaching a dam; so drop the matter before a dispute breaks out" (Proverbs 17:14).

Why argue with someone who is already set in his beliefs? Calmly plant your seeds of information in a person's mind and commit the issue to God, the only one who can cause a person to be receptive to an idea.

"Be kind to everyone." There is no need to be hostile, condescending, or disagreeable with anybody who does not share your view. What is motivating you toward such unkindness? Must you prove your opponent wrong to validate your self-worth? If the subject matter is not eternal and does not affect the quality of your life, learn to give others the luxury of having their own opinion without your ridicule.

"Able to teach." Be armed with knowledge and capable of presenting it coherently, but don't use it to beat others into submission to your view. Also understand that your ability to teach does not preclude you from being a learner.

"Not resentful." Resentment is nothing more than unresolved anger. Be honest about whatever hurts, disappointments, or disillusionments may be fueling your dogmatic attitude about a particular issue. Ask God for the courage and strength to confront and release it.

Creating a Peaceful Atmosphere

■ ■ ■ ■

Peace I leave with you; my peace I give you.
I do not give to you as the world gives.

JOHN 14:27

Have you ever spent time with someone who exudes peace no matter what is going on in her environment or even in her life? I had a former coworker, whom I will call Cynthia, who suffered domestic abuse at the hands of her alcoholic husband for more than 25 years before she left him. During this time, she also lost two of her five children to violent deaths, survived breast cancer, and experienced a host of other larger-than-life problems. When I first met her I was struck by the fact that nothing seemed to ruffle her feathers. Cynthia never complained about small issues like the broken copier, the freezing temperature in the office, or even her workload as the office manager. She was the epitome of peace, and it was apparent that she was not going to let anyone take it away from her. She set the tone for her environment no matter where she was.

What about you? How much peace do you exhibit? Let's start with your job. How well do you respond to the challenges of the day in your workplace? Are you always on edge or complaining? What is the appearance of your work area? Is it neat and orderly, or are there mountains of papers all around? I'm no neat freak, but I am a lot more peaceful and proficient when I'm not surrounded by things out of place. Disorder can be mentally distracting and stress-inducing. If your office is messy or you work in a space with messy people, you may find it necessary to temporarily work in a conference room or another area if you have a pressing project. If this isn't possible, try bundling papers with a giant rubber band and putting them out of sight as you work on one project at a time. Keep glass-top tables free of smudges. Live plants should be kept trimmed and free of dead or yellowing leaves. The sight of disorder can subconsciously erode your peace.

What about your overall demeanor? Are you always fuming over the mistakes of "dummies" and "idiots"? Have you learned to stop sweating the small stuff? Have you stopped to consider what a poor witness it is to not reflect peace, a fruit of the Spirit, in your life?

What about your daily commute? Do you get into your car with the intent of maintaining a peaceful atmosphere no matter what situations you encounter on the road? When was the last time you prayed for a bad or inconsiderate driver you really wished you could have given a premature trip to his eternal destination? Have you considered that you may be the only intercessor that person will have today? Do you create a peaceful atmosphere in your car by keeping the seats and floors free of clutter? Do you play relaxing music? The right music can be a great source of peace in any environment. When King Saul was tormented by an evil spirit, his servants told him, "Let us find a good musician to play the harp whenever the tormenting spirit troubles you. He will play soothing music, and you will soon be well again" (1 Samuel 16:16 NLT).

Regarding your domestic environment, I'm going to make an assumption that no matter what goes on outside, your home is your refuge and you guard its peace with all your might. You saturate the atmosphere with prayer each day, you communicate effectively, you are far from being selfish or insisting on your way, and you and your family "let the peace that comes from Christ rule in your hearts" (Colossians 3:15).

If you are indeed a model of peace, congratulations on allowing the Holy Spirit to do His work. Stay the course. Be the light that so shines that others will look at you and desire a relationship with our Lord.

Day 28

A Forward Focus

Remembering Past Victories

■ ■ ■ ■

The LORD who rescued me from the paw of
the lion and the paw of the bear will rescue
me from the hand of this Philistine.

1 SAMUEL 17:37

The ability to recall the past is one of the most powerful functions of
the brain. It can be both a blessing and a curse, depending on what you
choose to recall. Remembering brings the emotions of the past into the
"now" whether the event was positive or negative. Recalling old hurts,
offenses, disappointments, or failures will cause all of the emotions associated with them to rush to your mind to wreak havoc once again. Con-
versely, when you recall positive experiences, you rekindle the courage,
the joy, and the sense of accomplishment associated with the victory. You
can never underestimate the power of an experience to ignite faith. Such
was the case with David when he decided to fight Goliath. When King
Saul tried to discourage him from this seemingly impossible task, David
simply recalled a couple of his victorious moments.

> David said to Saul, "Your servant has been keeping his father's
> sheep. When a lion or a bear came and carried off a sheep from
> the flock, I went after it, struck it and rescued the sheep from
> its mouth. When it turned on me, I seized it by its hair, struck
> it and killed it. Your servant has killed both the lion and the

bear; this uncircumcised Philistine will be like one of them, because he has defied the armies of the living God" (1 Samuel 17:34-36).

From the parting of the Red Sea to the fall of Jericho, God had performed numerous miracles and mind-blowing feats on behalf of the Israelites, His chosen people. Moses had cautioned them about forgetting His mighty acts. "Remember well what the LORD your God did to Pharaoh and to all Egypt. You saw with your own eyes the great trials, the signs and wonders, the mighty hand and outstretched arm, with which the LORD your God brought you out. The LORD your God will do the same to all the peoples you now fear" (Deuteronomy 7:18-19).

Several years ago when I negotiated an unprecedented financing commitment for the construction of a mega-church sanctuary, I remember feeling inadequate from time to time as I met with the bankers regarding the highly complicated transaction. Some of the deal terms were new to the industry and foreign to me. I was concerned that my lack of familiarity would prove detrimental to the church. However, my anxiety was short-lived as I gained confidence each time I would recall that more than 14 years earlier, I had taken a job in an industry in which I had absolutely no experience. God had shown Himself strong and had allowed me to develop a reputation for being a great negotiator as well as being able to project future expenses with a high degree of accuracy. Because I had been so unfamiliar with the sophisticated operations, I knew beyond a shadow of a doubt that God had His angels working overtime on my behalf. It was a very humbling experience. It was then that I learned to just show up as prepared as I could be, but to expect the real answers, the brilliant stuff, to come from God.

If you have allowed Satan to give you "experience amnesia" and have forgotten those times of divine intervention in your life, try recalling someone else's testimony. Faith can come from more than one direction. Recall the good things God has done for your friends, acquaintances, coworkers, and even people you have heard about on the news. Miracles are exciting no matter who the recipient is. If He did it then, He can do it again.

Finally, do a study on the miracles in the Bible. Whenever I am feeling doubtful or unsure of my ability to overcome an obstacle, I read the story of David and Goliath. In fact, this section of this book was born out of those times. It is a good antidote for slaying any giant in your life.

Stop right now and recall a time or incident in which God brought you out of a difficult situation. Do you believe that He is the same yesterday, today, and forever?

The Pessimistic Attitude

■ ■ ■ ■

Tendency to expect the worst to happen

"Pessimistic Official Trampled to Death by Starving Mob!"

These words could have been the media headline that captured the events of that day when four lepers reported to Jehoram, king of Israel, that they had stumbled upon an abundant supply of food in a deserted enemy camp—enough to save the entire city of Samaria from starvation.

The saga had begun when the Syrian king Ben-Hadad laid siege to the city and cut off all food supplies. The ensuing famine was severe. Inflation was rampant. In order to survive, people were forced to eat donkey heads and use dove droppings for their cooking fires. Two mothers even agreed to eat each other's baby, but Mother Y reneged on the verbal contract after they'd eaten Mother X's baby (see 2 Kings 6:24–7:20).

King Jehoram, exasperated that God would allow such a situation to exist, decided to take his frustration out on God's prophet Elisha. Therefore, he ordered an official to go to Elisha's house and execute him. He even accompanied his official on the trip. However, when they arrived, Elisha prophesied that the famine would be over within 24 hours with food in abundance and at greatly reduced prices. Such an economic turnaround under any circumstance seemed unbelievable—especially to a pessimist.

> The officer on whose arm the king was leaning said to the man of God, "Look, even if the LORD should open the floodgates of heaven, could this happen?" "You will see it with your own eyes," answered Elijah, "but you will not eat any of it!" (2 Kings 7:2).

Shortly thereafter, four starving but optimistic lepers decided to go and beg for food in the enemy camp. But God had caused the Syrians to hear the sound of three invading armies approaching. All the soldiers had fled for their lives on foot, leaving horses, food, clothes, weapons, and the entire camp intact. The lepers were overjoyed. After indulging themselves, they reported their findings to the king. Ironically, he responded with the same pessimistic attitude exhibited by his official. (Could it be that by his behavior he had influenced his official's attitude?)

> The king got up in the night and said to his officers, "I will tell you what the Arameans have done to us. They know we are starving; so they have left the camp to hide in the countryside, thinking, 'They will surely come out, and then we will take them alive and get into the city'" (2 Kings 7:12).

The king dispatched a group to investigate, and they confirmed the lepers' story. The people were ecstatic—and hungry.

> Now the king had put the officer on whose arm he leaned in charge of the gate, and the people trampled him in the gateway, and he died, just as the man of God had foretold when the king came down to his house (2 Kings 7:17).

The official's pessimism cost him his life.

What about you? Is pessimism robbing you of life's fullness? Has a prolonged negative experience or a series of setbacks and disappointments caused you to see only the downside of every situation? Perhaps you're not even aware of your tendency to express hopelessness about the future, belittle your own abilities or that of others, refuse to take a calculated risk, resist personal growth opportunities, complain about the unfairness of life, or express powerlessness to make a difference in a particular circumstance. Do you want to conquer this attitude?

I'm reminded of the words of Dr. Paul Meier, popular Christian psychiatrist: "Attitudes are nothing more than habits of thoughts, and habits can be acquired. An action repeated becomes an attitude realized." The Word of God also provides practical advice for making a shift in your thinking. "Fix your thoughts on what is true, and honorable, and right, and pure, and lovely, and admirable. Think about things that are excellent and worthy of praise" (Philippians 4:8 NLT).

Overcoming pessimism requires more than a change in thinking; you must change your behavior. For starters, you must limit or eliminate your exposure to other pessimists. Begin to connect with optimistic people. Perhaps I should say *reconnect* because there is a good chance that many of your family members, coworkers, former friends, and others quietly distanced themselves from you as your pessimism continued to rear its head. Being with a pessimist is like having a skunk at your picnic.

You'll also want to try these additional strategies:

- Be candid with others about your quest to conquer pessimism. Give them permission to point out when you are being negative.

- Limit your exposure to negative input (media, movies, music).

- Volunteer to serve others who are less fortunate. Serving creates positive feelings and gives you a sense of value; it's also the right thing to do.

Yes, you can become an eternal optimist. Look for the good in every situation and always express faith that it is there! Remember the words of Harry S. Truman, thirty-third president of the United States: "The pessimist is one who makes difficulties of his opportunities and an optimist is one who makes opportunities of his difficulties."

Living on Purpose

■ ■ ■ ■

"For I know the plans I have for you," declares
the LORD, "plans to prosper you and not to harm
you, plans to give you hope and a future."

JEREMIAH 29:11

Nothing is more energizing and gratifying than walking in divine purpose—even when opposition or other circumstances threaten your pursuit. I worked as a corporate financial executive for over 30 years and every position I held was highly stressful and required me to work overtime. Many times (especially during the latter years) after a long and demanding day, I would come home at night feeling brain-dead. It seemed, however, that when I was the most fatigued, I would experience a surge of energy, clarity, and excitement as I sat down to my computer and begin to write the revelations of God. The Scriptures seemed to come alive with practical application. This is true even today when I'm at the height of fatigue. In those moments, I know beyond a shadow of a doubt that I am walking in my divine purpose. The fulfillment and personal satisfaction I feel are indescribable.

What about you? Are you walking in your divine purpose, or are you driving aimlessly on life's highway with no destination in mind? A purposeless existence is a major roadblock to emotional security. How can you walk with confidence and the complete assurance that God will cause you to succeed in your endeavors if you do not know for certain that you are on His path? Sadly, this is the state of too many of God's children. Unsure of their divine purpose, they trudge through their daily routines unfulfilled and frustrated. This is not the "abundant life" Jesus promised in John 10:10.

Because walking in purpose is so energizing, it seems that if someone is in doubt as to what his purpose is, a key question he would ask himself would be, "What energizes me and how can I use this energy to improve the life of others?" Surely, everyone has some level of passion for something. Of course, I have actually talked to people who say they do not have a passion for anything. I believe what they really mean is that they don't believe they could actually do what they really desire in their hearts.

Oh, that we would all experience the thrill of living life in our designated "lane." When driving the freeways, I often note the sign that says "Trucks Only." I immediately know that a certain portion of the highway has been set apart to facilitate the passage of large trucks and to avoid impeding the progress of cars. Consequently, all vehicles can reach their destination faster with each staying in their respective lanes. That's how it is when you become secure in your purpose. You stay in your lane. You don't get caught up trying to follow the path of others. You don't exit on Main Street just because it's the route Mary took to her destination (success). You begin to understand that your purpose may be found on Back Street—away from the mainstream.

Not understanding one's purpose can be a major roadblock to emotional security. For years, having grown up in a Pentecostal environment where speakers with highly emotional speaking styles tended to be the darlings, I battled insecurity about my teaching calling. I felt inadequate and apologetic when Pentecostal organizations invited me to speak. I always cautioned them that I was "just a teacher." Had I known I was walking in divine purpose, I wouldn't have felt the need to do that. My husband finally helped me to realize that my teaching gift is the "lane" God has ordained for me. I don't have to emulate anyone else's style. God knows what each of His children needs. Many are simply more receptive to particular styles of speaking. If a speaker chooses to "honk the horn" while she is driving, there is no need for me to do so just because it seems to get everyone's attention. As in the truck example cited earlier, I have to respect what she does in her lane and not be critical of nor intimidated by her.

We must also be careful to *stay* in our lane by guarding against distractions. Jesus stayed in His lane and refused to let anyone pull Him away from His primary purpose. One day while He was teaching, He was interrupted with a request that would have sidetracked Him from His purpose.

"Someone in the crowd said to him, 'Teacher, tell my brother to divide the inheritance with me.' Jesus replied, 'Man, who appointed me a judge or an arbiter between you?'" (Luke 12:13-14). In essence, Jesus was saying, "Look, I'm not about to get distracted by conducting an arbitration hearing between you two. That's not part of My purpose for being here on earth."

Now, I have to confess that I find it hard to resist the temptation to become involved in matters that are not part of what God has called me to do. In the past I have often rescued people to their detriment—and mine. I am still learning to distinguish between being "capable" and being "called."

Even up to the day that Jesus gave His life on the cross, there were still many sick people needing healing, bound people needing deliverance, and a myriad of other impossible situations demanding His attention. However, despite these unresolved circumstances, He confidently gave His heavenly Father this report on His ministry: "I brought glory to you here on earth by completing the work *you* gave me to do" (John 17:4 NLT, emphasis added). He refused to let Satan, His disciples, well-meaning family members, needy people, or anyone else distract Him from His purpose.

What about you? Are you clear about your divine purpose? Are you ardently pursuing it? If you do not yet know what it is, could it be that you are approaching your search from the perspective of how it will enhance *your* life rather than the lives of others? Think about it.

Day 29

Pressing Toward the Mark

Refusing to Be Deterred

■ ■ ■ ■

*You are not able to go out against this Philistine
and fight him; you are only a young man, and
he has been a warrior from his youth.*

1 Samuel 17:33

There will always be people who will try to prevent or discourage you
from killing your giant of insecurity or any other giant in your life. Their
resistance could be due to the fact that "misery loves company," or they are
projecting their lack of faith onto you, or they have any other reasons to
keep you locked in your cell of inadequacy. Whatever the intention, you
may find that you have to stand alone in your quest.

David met with discouragement as soon as he came to the battlefield
and asked why everyone was running from Goliath. His oldest brother,
Eliab, accused him of being a conceited show-off. "'Now what have I
done?' said David. 'Can't I even speak?' *He then turned away to someone else* and brought up the same matter" (1 Samuel 17:29-30, emphasis
added). David's response to Eliab's criticism represents a key strategy in
dealing with discouragers. It reminds me of my elders in the South. When
they wanted to let someone know they were ignoring his comments, they
would say, "I'm not studin' you!" To study was to give something careful
thought and consideration. When David turned from Eliab to speak to
the other men, he was in essence saying to him, "I'm not studin' you! I'm

not giving your accusation careful thought and consideration." We can easily fall into the trap of "studying" the words of a discourager.

There was more discouragement David had to face. Even King Saul cautioned him against confronting Goliath. "David said to Saul, 'Let no one lose heart on account of this Philistine; your servant will go and fight him.' Saul replied, 'You are not able to go out against this Philistine and fight him; you are only a young man, and he has been a warrior from his youth'" (1 Samuel 17:32-33).

David, however, was not concerned about how much experience Goliath had because David knew that God was all-powerful. How tragic it is when we limit our faith to only what we can see or figure out. Believing we are inadequate for a task is to engage in self-centeredness. We begin to focus on what we perceive our own capabilities to be apart from God. This independent mindset shuts Him out of the equation and ignores the fact that His strength is made perfect in weakness. God doesn't call the qualified; He qualifies the called.

If you are a Christian, there is a good chance that some of your resistance will come from those who are heirs to the same promises you claim. Like Eliab (whose name meant "God is my Father"), God's children can be resentful or envious of your desire to conquer your giant. You must make an independent decision to persevere until you have the victory.

Let's say you are insecure about speaking in public, not only because of your noticeably Southern accent, but also because you need to shed more than a few pounds. Notwithstanding, you have a great command of English and the church needs volunteers in this area of ministry for the weekly announcements. You press past your own self-criticism and decide to go for it. However, you make the mistake of telling your shy, plump friend Betty. To your disappointment, Betty discourages you from participating. "Girl, they are going to call you 'country' if you get up there with that Southern drawl. And have you noticed how thin those announcement clerks are? It must be an unwritten requirement. I'll bet you'll be buying some fancier clothes too. You see how sophisticated they all dress—just because they have to sit on the platform when it's their turn to make announcements. Humph!"

How would you reply to Betty's comments? Would you say, "Get thee behind me, Satan. I have a giant to kill"? Well, not really. Even though you understand what is motivating her comments, you must still respond in love.

"Betty, I'm aware of all of the *facts*. The *truth*, however, is that I feel that God wants me to serve in this capacity, so I'm going for it. He can handle the rest."

You cannot afford to allow another person's input, which emanates from their insecurity, to reinforce your own. You have to handle such discouragers the same way you would handle any toxic substance: Eliminate or limit your exposure. When you must come into contact with them, protect yourself with the proper attire—that is, the whole armor of God (see Ephesians 6:11-18).

Nehemiah's enemies tried every trick in the book to deter him from rebuilding the wall of the city of Jerusalem, which lay in ruins. Notice how he handled their opposition.

> Sanballat and Geshem sent me this message: "Come, let us meet together in one of the villages on the plain of Ono." But they were scheming to harm me; so I sent messengers to them with this reply: "I am carrying on a great project and cannot go down. Why should the work stop while I leave it and go down to you?" Four times they sent me the same message, and each time I gave them the same answer (Nehemiah 6:2-4).

Nehemiah remained steadfast despite their efforts to deter him. Sometimes you have to become a broken record when you really mean business about slaying your giant. You must be willing to take the put-downs, the envy, the distractions, the discouraging words, and all other opposition.

Has anyone tried to discourage you from slaying your giant? How have you responded?

Resisting Intimidation

■ ■ ■ ■

"Come here," he said, "and I'll give your flesh
to the birds and the wild animals!"

1 SAMUEL 17:44

Goliath towered over David as he made his threats. Although David had to look up at him when he responded, spiritually he was looking down upon him. He looked at the giant through the eyes of his omnipotent

God, who sits high, looks low, and conquers all. It was God Himself who asked the prophet Jeremiah, "I am the LORD, the God of all mankind. Is anything too hard for me?" (Jeremiah 32:27).

David didn't shrink back when Goliath threatened to feed him to the birds. He wasn't intimidated. To intimidate is to instill fear. Notice how conspicuously the word *timid* appears in the word in*timid*ate? Satan wants the giant in our lives to instill fear in our hearts so that it can continue to subdue us and to keep us from going forward.

David believed God. "You come against me with sword and spear and javelin, but I come against you in the name of the LORD Almighty, the God of the armies of Israel, whom you have defied" (1 Samuel 17:45).

When battling the giant of insecurity, intimidation is most likely to come from your own erroneous assessment of your value or abilities. You can literally *think* yourself into a state of apprehension, fearfulness, and unworthiness.

Take a cartoon segment on Charlie Brown and Linus. They are having lunch at school and Charlie Brown confides to Linus that he doesn't feel good enough to approach a certain young lady. He laments, "I can't talk to that little red-haired girl because she's something and I'm nothing. Now, if I were something and she were nothing, I could talk to her, or if she were something and I were something, then I could talk to her, or if she were nothing and I were nothing, I also could talk to her...But she's something and I'm nothing, so I can't talk to her." Linus, having listened intently to his confession of his insecurity, responds, "For a nothing, Charlie Brown, you're really something." Charlie Brown had allowed the redhead's beauty to intimidate him and force him to the sidelines.

I cannot remember a time in my adult life when I have been too fearful to approach someone others have deemed important or intimidating. I refuse to believe that anybody is inherently better than I am simply because he is wealthier, renowned, or can claim any other distinction. I endeavor to keep a "God perspective" when interacting with everybody. To Him, we are all mere flesh made from the dust of the earth. Yes, He gives some greater responsibilities, resources, and exposure, but He doesn't play favorites. We are all the same in His eyes. As the old saying goes, "The ground is level at the foot of the cross."

David wasn't going to stand for Goliath's intimidation; he knew how to talk back.

David said to the Philistine, "*This day* the LORD will deliver you into my hands, and I'll strike you down and cut off your head. *This very day* I will give the carcasses of the Philistine army to the birds and wild animals, and the whole world will know that there is a God in Israel. All those gathered here will know that it is not by sword or spear that the LORD saves; for the battle is the LORD's, and He will give all of you into our hands" (1 Samuel 17:46-47, emphasis added). What a great retort to Goliath's threats!

Are you ready to declare to your giant that today is the day of its demise? Whether it is the giant of insecurity, alcoholism, an unruly tongue, or a host of other self-defeating behaviors, the giant must go. You can decide to defeat him today.

Is there a person or situation that intimidates you? What declaration from the Scriptures will you make to "talk back" to your giant?

Running Toward the Giant

■ ■ ■ ■

As the Philistine moved closer to attack him, David
ran quickly toward the battle line to meet him.

1 SAMUEL 17:48

Are you ready to grab your sword of faith and behead that giant that has been intimidating you? Your best strategy will always be to attack a giant before it has a chance to get the best of you. Eleanor Roosevelt said, "You gain strength, courage, and confidence by every experience in which you really stop to look fear in the face."

Whether real or imagined, all threats are perceived as a potential for loss. It may be the loss of recognition, loss of favor, loss of affection, or even the loss of a desired relationship. Freedom begins when we stop and make an honest confession of the loss we really fear.

Identifying your real fears is the first step toward breaking free of the giant of insecurity. To do this, you must go through the process of peeling the "fear onion" to get to the core of your anxiety or sense of inadequacy. Depending on your history of being honest with yourself, you may have to peel back a lot more layers than expected.

When I served in a key financial position for a certain corporation, I knew the company's board of directors held me in esteem as a competent professional. I took pains to maintain my image in their eyes. During a particular board meeting, one of the members presented a proposal for investment of the organization's idle funds. She stated that we could probably get a much higher return than we were realizing with our current strategy. As she continued to explain her recommendation, I felt anxiety begin to rear its ugly head. Having just begun my study on insecurity only days before, I was ready to defy and reject its intrusion in my life. Now I saw that it was not going to be easy.

The more she explained her proposal, the more Satan assaulted my mind. *Why hadn't I presented that idea? Now they're going to think that I'm not so bright after all. Why didn't she run the idea by me first before presenting it to the board?* I brought my imaginations to a screeching halt and asked myself: "What do I fear?" The answer was quick and painful. I feared the loss of their esteem for me. I feared that the accolades I received at each board meeting would cease. God forbid! I loved those praises. I worked many uncompensated hours to be excellent—and, yes, to be recognized for being so. Now here was someone threatening my position on the pedestal. And to boot, the presenter did not even have a financial background.

Like Saul when he felt threatened with the loss of his kingdom to David, I felt anger toward this woman. However, unlike Saul, I was not going to allow insecurity to run amok in my life. I had learned from his mistake. I took a deep breath and silently recited 2 Corinthians 10:5: "Casting down arguments and every high thing that exalts itself against the knowledge of God, bringing every thought into captivity to the obedience of Christ" (NKJV). My thoughts were running wild. I quickly reined them in. I knew that acknowledging my real fear would put me on the fast track to freedom. *So what that she presented a good plan to maximize our return on idle cash?* I mused. How in the world could that impact the quality of my life? Unless, of course, my life was wrapped up in trying to be the "Wonder Woman" who always had the answer to every problem.

By suggesting to me that a loss of some kind was imminent, Satan had already planted the seed of insecurity. However, having acknowledged my core fear, I quickly derailed his plan. This is the strategy we must use on thoughts of insecurity; we must attack them at an early stage with proactive, aggressive action.

David did not stand there and wait for the approaching giant to subdue him. "As the Philistine moved closer to attack him, David ran quickly toward the battle line to meet him. Reaching into his bag and taking out a stone, he slung it and struck the Philistine on the forehead. The stone sank into his forehead, and he fell facedown on the ground" (1 Samuel 17:48-49). No more dialogue. The giant had to die.

Thankfully the battle we fight with the giant of insecurity is not one we fight alone. God wants to fight it for us. As Hanani told King Asa, "The eyes of the LORD range throughout the earth to strengthen those whose hearts are fully committed to him" (2 Chronicles 16:9). All that He wants from us is a commitment.

Again, the victory begins when we start to get real about what we fear and the loss that we dread. Answering the right questions can be like using a surgeon's scalpel in getting to the root of your fears. Do not lie to yourself. It's time to be honest. It is time to slay the giant of insecurity. Try to answer the questions below to get started on "peeling the onion."

What situation or setting causes you to feel insecure? What do you really fear? Is there a rational basis for this fear? How does this insecurity cause you to behave? Is this behavior godly? If not, what behavior do you think God would consider appropriate?

Even though it could be a bit difficult, this exercise can also be very cathartic and liberating. The best benefit of it is that you get to put the problem out in the open, confront it, and develop a plan for overcoming it. Dale Carnegie admonished, "Do the thing you fear to do and keep on doing it. That is the quickest and surest way ever yet discovered to conquer fear."

Day 30

Embracing the Good Life

Conquering Self-Sabotaging Behavior

■ ■ ■ ■

*The prudent see danger and take refuge, but
the simple keep going and pay the penalty.*

PROVERBS 27:12

Are you your own worst enemy—your biggest stressor? Do you engage in behavior that often leads to a stress-producing incident? Listed below are several behaviors or situations that you would do well to consider eliminating from your daily routine:

- Some women carry large purses that contain everything that they will need from sunrise to sunset. Trying to locate an item in it—particularly in a rush—can be quite stressful. To break the "everything but the kitchen sink" habit, note how often you actually use each item in your purse each day. If the answer is never, then it may be a good candidate for leaving at home. Try carrying only the basics, such as your wallet, lipstick, and keys.

- Do you find yourself driving down the freeway and fumbling for your cell phone when you get a call? Why not just make a habit of putting the phone in an easily accessible spot the minute you get in the car?

- Do you shop with your purse open as if to say to a would-be purse snatcher, "Welcome. Come on in"? Further, an open purse allows items to fall out of it. I live in a hilly area, and I'm always spilling the contents of my purse when I go down the hills. This is frustrating, but whom can I blame for self-sabotage?

- How peaceful are your travel preparations? Because I travel a lot, I keep duplicate items of toiletries packed in my suitcase, and therefore have no need to run around looking for them at the last minute. In the past, I have forgotten almost every item at one time or another that I considered "essential." Now, I have a preprinted packing checklist that sets forth everything I will need. I print out a copy for each trip. The list is categorized by business, personal grooming, exercise gear, books/products, and so forth. It has made getting out of the house for my trips a lot less stressful.

- How many times have you lost your car in a parking lot or structure? Wherever I park now, the first thing I note is my parking location. I recite it several times as I leave the car. I once was only minutes away from reporting my car stolen after having looked for it for what seemed like hours. I finally located it on a floor of the parking structure where most of the cars had left. No more of this stressful madness for me.

- If you've entered that forgetful period in your life, when you go out, look around you when you get up to be sure you've collected all your belongings. Constantly losing your items can cause quite a bit of stress for you and your companions.

- At home, always have a designated place for the things you need to use often. I keep a bowl or a basket by the door for keys, a vitamin carousel that stays in a set place, a closet organized in a manner such that the things I can wear currently are positioned in the front to avoid my going through the entire closet each time I have to get dressed.

- Do not take the cordless phone from the room where the base is located. It may be worth your sanity to have a phone in each room.

- If you wear reading glasses but can't keep up with them, buy several pairs and designate each one for a particular location. Be diligent about keeping them in their appointed places.

- Do you realistically plan for traffic or things not going as scheduled? Are your assumptions too optimistic as to how long it will take to complete a task or drive to an appointment? The truth of the matter is that I could indeed do things within the bounds of my optimistic time frame if I were the only person on the planet. However, things happen. Rather than bemoaning certain realities, you simply need to anticipate them.

Try to reduce most of your daily activities to a routine. Good planning and forethought are critical to minimizing self-caused stress. They will not reduce you to a life of boredom but rather will give you more time to plan something exciting and fulfilling.

Reaping the Reward

■ ■ ■ ■

What will be done for the man who kills this
Philistine and removes this disgrace from Israel?

1 SAMUEL 17:26

Slaying any giant in your life has its rewards. When David first came to the battlefield and saw God's people running from the uncircumcised Philistine, he immediately wanted to know what his reward would be for killing him. The men responded, "The king will give great wealth to the man who kills him. He will also give him his daughter in marriage and will exempt his family from taxes in Israel" (1 Samuel 17:25). I'm certain these three rewards provided a great incentive to slay the giant. But, of course, it was also part of David's destiny to do so. Let's look at some tangible and intangible rewards of slaying the giant of insecurity.

Slaying the giant of insecurity frees you from the bonds of inadequacy that have kept you from pursuing your dreams. Let's say your insecurity is in the area of public speaking and that there is a high-paying position available in your firm that would require you to make formal presentations on a regular basis. You know the material cold, but the thought of getting up even in front of a small group causes knots to form in your stomach. But you really could use the increase in pay. What do you do? Well, don't just sit there and squander an opportunity. Remember that confidence is rooted in knowledge. If you have the technical competence, you're halfway to your goal already. Apply for the job. Believe that God will show Himself strong and help you with your presentations. In the meantime, while you are walking by faith, join a local Toastmasters group, take a public speaking class at the local college, or buy tapes or CDs that give tips for overcoming stage fright. Run toward the giant.

I have had several employees during the course of my professional career that battled insecurity. From time to time I have selected a few to be the target of my "tough love" and demanded a much higher level of performance because I knew they had the potential. Many have come back and reported their success and have thanked me for believing in them and pushing them beyond their comfort zones. I am committed to not only slaying the giants in my life but also helping others to slay their giants. God's children have no excuse for living with insecurity when He has promised us that we can do all things through Him who strengthens us.

One of the most significant intangible rewards of slaying a giant is the inspiration it gives others to slay their own giants. Nobody in King Saul's army had ever killed a giant. By contrast, after David killed Goliath, four other men, including his nephew, Jonathan, killed the giants that rose up against the Israelites. I read with great satisfaction and amusement the account of Jonathan's encounter with a giant:

> In still another battle, which took place at Gath, there was a huge man with six fingers on each hand and six toes on each foot—twenty-four in all. He also was descended from Rapha. When he taunted Israel, Jonathan son of Shimeah, David's brother, killed him (2 Samuel 21:20-21).

What a marked contrast between how Israel dealt with a giant *before* David killed Goliath and the courage they developed *after* he killed him. Notice in the passage above that nobody is running away. There is also a conspicuous absence of fanfare in the telling of this event. There is no blow-by-blow account of the dialogue that transpired between Jonathan and the giant as there was with David and Goliath. The Bible simply states that when the giant taunted Israel, Jonathan "killed him." David had set a new standard.

Until 1954 no one had ever run a mile in under four minutes. It was the unconquerable giant in the runners' world during that time. Most people assumed it was virtually impossible for a human being to accomplish such a feat; that is, everyone except Roger Bannister. The 25-year-old British medical student used his medical knowledge to give him as much help as possible. He also researched mechanical aspects of running and used scientific training methods. On May 6, 1954, at an Oxford University track meet, Roger completed the distance in three minutes and 59.4 seconds. He had slain the giant. Unfortunately, Roger never won an Olympic medal, for Australian John Landy broke his record within two months, proving that the four-minute mile was as much a psychological as a physical barrier. Notwithstanding, Bannister had set the standard.

Mount Everest is the highest peak on earth above sea level, rising approximately 5.5 miles. A normal expedition lasts 60 to 90 days. In the first half of the twentieth century, many people had attacked the formidable mountain. It was the unconquerable giant in the world of mountain climbers. On May 29, 1953, Edmund Hillary and his Sherpa guide, Tenzing Norgay, were the first humans to reach the summit. Hillary was knighted for his feat. Since then, approximately 1,000 climbers, ranging from age 16 to 60, have completed the expedition.

David, Bannister, and Hillary all conquered giants of their day and inspired others to match or excel their feats.

We do ourselves and others a disservice when we run from our giants. We need to stop being afraid of tackling hard tasks. If God did it then, He can do it again.

What person do you admire for being the first to accomplish a certain feat? Do you dream of doing something that no one else has ever done? Prayerfully consider why God continues to let you dream. Could it be that someone is waiting for you to set the standard in this area?

Walking in Victory

■ ■ ■ ■

Overwhelming victory is ours through Christ, who loved us.

ROMANS 8:37

Sometimes you have to behave your way to victory. Once you have sought the Lord and accepted by faith that He has delivered you from your fears, you must begin to model the behavior of a secure person. Emotions follow actions. You will begin to feel more secure when you start to engage in secure behavior. Just as David ran toward the physically intimidating Philistine giant, so must we run toward the emotionally intimidating giant of insecurity. We must not take an ostrich-like approach and pretend that insecurity is not there; we cannot be healed from that which we conceal. We must confess our insecurity and conquer it with the Word of God.

Amassing worldly trappings, such as designer clothes, fancy cars, loads of money, or a list of influential friends, will be as ineffective in curing insecurity as a putting a Band-Aid on a cancerous limb. Facades of confidence are just that—facades; they do not have the power to defeat insecurity. We must slay this giant with spiritual weapons.

The principles of overcoming insecurity are as simple as ABC:

- A—Acknowledge your core fear. Self-deception will keep you in the pit of insecurity.

- B—Believe that God can and will deliver you. Nothing is too hard for Him.

- C—Change your thoughts. Behavior follows belief. Cast down every thought of inadequacy and all other security-robbing imaginations.

These steps are simple but not easy. You must become like the remora fish that attaches itself to the powerful shark and exists by staying connected. You must stay connected to the omnipotent, omniscient, and omnipresent God. Daily confess, "I am surrounded with the favor of God. I am safe, sure, sufficient. I am secure."

South African president Nelson Mandela, in his 1994 inaugural address, eloquently stated,

Our deepest fear is not that we are inadequate. Our deepest fear is that we are powerful beyond measure. It is our light, not our darkness that frightens us. We ask ourselves, who am I to be brilliant, gorgeous, talented, and fabulous? Actually, who are we not to be? You are a child of God. Your playing small doesn't serve the world. There's nothing enlightened about shrinking so that other people won't feel insecure around you. We were born to make manifest the glory of God that is within us. It's not just in some of us; it's in everyone. And as we let our own light shine, we unconsciously give other people permission to do the same. As we are liberated from our own fears, our presence automatically liberates others.

The following healing prayer will help you resist thoughts of insecurity and keep you on the path to being the confident person you are destined to be.

■ ■ ■ ■

Father, I come boldly before Your throne of grace to obtain mercy and find grace for deliverance. I stand on Your Word that assures me that You are able to make all of Your grace abound toward me so that I will always have all sufficiency in all things and will abound in every good work. I cast down every thought of inadequacy and every imagination that rises up against what Your Word says about who I am and what I can do.

I resist any anxiety over the possibility of losing a social, professional, or other position, or a desired relationship. I know that no one can thwart Your purpose for my life. You, O Lord, have sealed my destiny and You guard all that is mine.

Thank You, Father, for my unchangeable physical features (height, race, hair, complexion, etc.). I repent for all of the times I rejected Your design and allowed insecurity to creep in because of worldly standards. I know, according to Your Word, that You deliberately shaped me in the womb to be Your servant. Therefore, I rest and rejoice in the truth that I am designed for my destiny and am perfect for my purpose.

Because of Your grace, I walk neither in self-doubt nor in self-confidence because I know that apart from You I can do absolutely nothing. Therefore, my eyes are on You alone to do exceedingly, abundantly above all that I could ask or think according to Your power that works in me.

I thank You that as I have prayed, You have heard me and delivered me from all my fears; they no longer have any power over my life.

Thank You for the confidence that is mine because I am connected to You, my all-powerful, all-knowing, and always-present Father. In the name of Jesus Christ, I pray. Amen.

Epilogue

■■■■

Now that you have learned to name and control your emotions and you've met like-minded people throughout these pages, consider your options—and, yes, you do have options. With each "emotional challenge" you can chose not to react at all or to establish a new normal, a new way of responding that will improve the quality of your life.

You can start by changing your outlook. Make it a habit to embrace a divine perspective. Before you react to any situation, believe that all things are working together for your good and for a divine purpose. When you're in a right relationship with God, such a mindset will guard your mental well-being. You can never be a victim, you can never be inadequate, and you can never harbor a wrong attitude when you are convinced that in the final analysis God is up to something good on your behalf.

Hopefully, the preceding chapters have given you not only a biblical foundation but some practical tools on bringing your emotions under control. Always challenge the core beliefs about God and who you are in Him that give rise to your disturbing thoughts and negative emotions. Learn to recognize Satan's lies. Yes, many erroneous assumptions and irrational ideas will continue to bombard your thoughts from time to time. Know that they are false—even if you do indeed see a modicum of reality peeking through. That's what makes a lie palatable—that tiny element of reality! The apostle Paul left us with the only antidote to this dilemma: "Casting down imaginations, and every high thing that exalteth itself against the knowledge of God, and bringing into captivity every thought to the obedience of Christ" (2 Corinthians 10:5 KJV).

Finally, give yourself a break when you do not respond perfectly in every situation and the negative emotions seem to prevail. That's why

God sent the Holy Spirit—to help you. That's why Jesus sits at the right hand of the Father—to make intercession for you. Don't set yourself up for a lifetime of failure. Say goodbye to debilitating stress, wrong attitudes, and insecurity. Say hello to peace, positivity, and power over erroneous thinking.

Deborah Smith Pegues is an experienced certified public accountant, a Bible teacher, an inspiring motivator, and a certified behavioral consultant specializing in understanding personality temperaments. As well as the bestselling *30 Days to Taming Your Tongue* (more than 500,000 sold), she has authored *30 Days to Taming Your Finances* and *30 Days to Taming Your Stress*. She and her husband, Darnell, have been married since 1979 and make their home in California.

For speaking engagements, please contact the author at:

The Pegues Group
P.O. Box 56382
Los Angeles, California 90056
(323) 293-5861

or

E-mail: deborah @confrontingissues.com
www.confrontingissues.com

To learn more about Harvest House books and
to read sample chapters, log on to our website:

www.harvesthousepublishers.com

HARVEST HOUSE PUBLISHERS
EUGENE, OREGON